*This book is for Michael*

# CONTENTS

# INTRODUCTION

AMATEUR HISTORIANS too often *do* local history, or find themselves involved with local history, without considering just what history is all about. It is easy to accept local history as it has often been done in the past—undefined, lacking in context, in perspective, in judgment—without realizing its larger potential. Because history is in the public domain; because its content is frequently cited by a variety of people who are not themselves historians; because history is so often *used* by journalists, politicians, orators, preachers, and numerous others; history appears to be accessible to anyone with time and interest to invest. In this way, history is totally unlike the medical arts: medicine does not invite amateur participation, nor would the public long tolerate an amateur doctor or dentist. The past, however, belongs to us all; the language of history is the language we speak. Historical methods—except, perhaps, for recent forays by highly sophisticated historians into mathematical and statistical history—depend upon intelligence and common sense, and most history is not cloaked from view by an arcane jargon or methodology too complex for anyone who is interested but not formally trained to understand. Moreover, almost anyone can pick up a volume of history and profit by reading it. This very accessibility of the past permits anyone with any purpose to become involved with it. Local history is, of course, the most accessible of all history, for it is closest to home.

A number of writers have set up formulas to be followed when writing, researching, or presenting local history: what to do and how to do it. Other writers have set down lists of rules for local historians,

1

telling them—us—to write clearly, to use footnotes, to include maps, and the like. These writers address local history and local historians in a prescriptive fashion, believing it their duty to dictate steps to follow, to present a guide showing how history ought to be done. All of this literature is helpful, in one way or another. What is lacking in those books and articles is the essential issue of thinking about local history, taking the time to consider what one does and why and what local history in all its forms means to the historian, to the public, and to our sense of who we are.

This book in no way duplicates those other efforts; these essays do not present, much less dictate, a plan for success. Rather, they attempt to consider what it is we do and the conditions and traditions in which we labor—amateurs in a field of endeavor where there are highly trained and talented professionals and where there has developed a variety of sophisticated methodologies.

The word "amateur" itself has in our time come to mean one whose performance is less than the very best. "It was an amateur effort," some might say after a poorly produced play; or "Not bad—for an amateur," meaning that excellence was never to be expected in the first place. The word "amateur" comes, however, from the Latin *amator,* meaning "to love." An amateur historian loves history, both the past itself and the study of the past. Such a person tends to be known as a "history buff"—not one who runs about clothed in nothing but historical knowledge, but one who buffs up, polishes up, reads up on historical events. If the individual specializes, then he or she might be known as a "railroad buff." An amateur who wants to know about the past of a particular area is called, for better or worse, a "local historian"—or sometimes a "little old lady in tennis shoes."

Amateur ornithologists—bird watchers—and others share this appellation with us, but most often "little old lady in tennis shoes" means a local historian—be that person a male or female, old or not. The term annoys many people, as does the word "amateur." The English journal published by the British Association for Local History even changed its name in 1968 from *The Amateur Historian* to *The Local Historian.*[1]

A number of scholars have written about the word "amateur" and about amateur status. Jacob Burckhardt, the great Swiss historian, commented that the meaning of the word had been spoiled because of the arts: artists must be either masters or else nothing; and they must dedicate their lives to art, for the arts demand perfection. Edward Shils, an American sociologist, cautions that "to be an amateur is a derogatory status. It is more acceptable among the rich to be an idler with inherited wealth than it is to be a serious intellectual amateur." Shils believes that because of this attitude, anyone who is seriously involved with the pursuit of knowledge seeks the shelter of the academy.[2] As we progress through these essays, I think you will see that we can substitute "professional organization" for "academy," because historians of all sorts who find themselves doing history outside of a university setting customarily seek affiliation within some organizational framework.[3]

One attack on the distinction between amateur and professional historians comes from the editor of *CHAT,* the newsletter of the County Historians Association of New York:

I guess the term that rankles . . . is "Professional Historian," versus "Amateur Historian," meaning US! Some of us who have been around a decade or so have to smile at the professor who has just "discovered" local history materials and methods we have been using, lo, these many years, and his patronizing attitudes. I opt for the term: "Academic Historians" to distinguish those in the institutions of higher learning, but even that isn't strictly correct, as many of us have dwelt among the halls of higher learning, even as they. In my county, the majority of our historians are former teachers. And all of us know that having a degree doesn't amount to a hill of beans versus the education gained in the School of Experience. If there were degrees given out in Masters of Local History, I suspect that most of us would be able to pass the equivalency examination with flying colors.[4]

The writer complains that grants, prizes, and recognition are all geared to the academic historian, whereas amateurs suffer from a poor image, have difficulty getting their work published, and lack opportunities that are routine for those in the universities. Life for academic historians is not quite so rosy as intimated here: some professional historians have trouble getting published and are not lavished with grants and awards. Other historians find themselves outside an academic setting by personal choice or because of the tight job market. We find highly trained historians working in publishing, at historical associations, and as historians in government or business.

In a somewhat gentler tone, D. G. Edwards, writing in *The Local Historian,* also tackles the distinction between amateur and professional. In answer to the question, "Who is the amateur and who the professional?" he wrote:

I would suggest that the only basic difference is that the latter makes a career of the subject and has been specifically trained for it. The good amateur must be just as "professional" in his approach—he has to be critical, analytical, and imaginative. . . .[5]

I do not expect this book to alter the status of the amateur historian; but in it I intend to discuss why this situation exists, some of the ways we local historians might begin to improve our image, and how we communicate local history to the public.

To begin, let me venture a definition of local history, for local history lends itself to many interpretations. My preference is for a descriptive phrase that allows for flexibility. I take issue with the rather outmoded English view that local history is the study of the origin, growth, and decline of communities. Promoted in the late 1950s and 1960s by English scholars associated with Leicester University, this definition confines one to identifying a particular community and then following a particular course to determine its past. Nor do I believe that local history is only national history writ small, for such a view would place me in the position of looking only for that which can be found in the larger historical picture while ignoring the special rhythms and themes that emerge in my particular locale.

I see local history as the study of past events, or of people or groups, in a given geographic area—a study based on a wide variety of documentary evidence and placed in a comparative context that should be both regional and national. Such study ought to be accomplished by a historian using methods appropriate to the topic under consideration, while following general rules of historical inquiry: open-mindedness, honesty, accountability, and accuracy. This definition legitimizes all sorts of research projects. Local history is, at its heart—as is history itself—the study of the human condition in and through time. We look for an understanding of our past. If that past is relevant to understanding our present or future condition, that is all to the good, but this need not be our only goal. Doing local history is a process of learning, and it is about explaining causes—the how, and the why, of the past.

Local history is, despite its limited geographical focus, a broad field of inquiry: it is the political, social, and economic history of a community, and religious and intellectual history, too. It is a place to look for individual reactions to historical events and the arena in which to practice demographic investigation. Local history is the place to hear women's voices, find information about child-rearing practices, ask questions related to education, leisure, and privacy. Local history allows us to look at town planning and our domestic architecture. It begs for studies of how we have lived in the past, in this particular place, and it offers an opportunity to study group biography, leadership, philanthropy, crime, and gender. Local history is the study of who remained in a community and who left— and why.

Local history is the framework in which to practice cultural history in an attempt to understand an area's distinctive style. The local historian has, in addition to documents, objects that add material culture to the historian's "bag of tricks": architecture, clothing, products of local manufacture, and the environment all become important. The tools and the products of folklore and folklife studies—sometimes confused with local history—can illuminate the story of local history. Local history encompasses many forms of history, and it uses a variety of historical methods—from oral to statistical to literary.

There is no standard apprenticeship that one must follow in order to research and write history. An artist, master painter or one of the Sunday variety, must learn to mix colors, understand perspective, and think about selection—what to put in a painting and what to leave out. These same problems, or variations on them, occur in the historical context also, but few amateurs take the time to focus on anything but the immediate story to be told. Most amateurs become so engrossed with the job of research and the pleasure of writing up materials that they generally fail to identify questions that the discipline of history asks, much less discuss or consider appropriate ways of finding answers. Blame for this situation can easily be allocated. Many local historians fail to read historical literature from outside their own locales or areas of special interest. For example, one well-regarded local historian, in a small township located twenty miles away from a fair-sized American city, insists that a study of nineteenth-century religion in the nearby urban area is not of interest or importance to her own community. She cannot be moved to read the new book. This is not an extreme or uncommon situation, nor is the local historian involved a lazy woman. She simply does not see that the history of a nearby community may be relevant to the history of *her* community. She does not read history for ideas or for the methodology employed; she simply wants "to know" what happened in her community.

But! More blame than this remains to be distributed, for professional historians in the United States have almost totally ignored their responsibility to the amateurs who also labor in Clio's fields. With some exceptions, and until quite recently, professional historians have ignored local historians, have failed to share in the study of local history or to provide leadership, and have disparaged amateur efforts and most amateur activities. This situation is different in different parts of the country; some state historical associations have long been the meeting place for various types of historians, and some states have networks of local and professional historians that function on behalf of their areas' history. Yet how many academic historians belong to the local historical societies in their own hometowns? More now, perhaps, than did several years ago, but unless they are brought in especially to help for a particular reason, many are disengaged from local groups. Academic historians have rarely taught, written for, or talked with amateurs. I can hear cries of protest from academe already. I know the many ways in which the local historian is vulnerable to honest and telling criticism. Still, rather than attempt to upgrade or improve, to encourage the work of local historians, by and large most professional historians have simply thrown up their hands and turned their backs. The responsibility that I am meting out belongs squarely in both camps.

Instead of rehashing old difficulties, however, I prefer to look forward, to attempt some mutual understanding—and ultimately cooperation—between amateur and professional historians. Since the 1960s, the nature of academic social history has changed. Local studies, using documentary materials in the community, are being pursued by graduate students everywhere. One result has been the publication of articles and books that should have import for and impact on amateur historians. This development has also meant that for the first time in a great while, academic historians are coming into contact with local historians. More and more academic historians attend local history conferences as participants, more and more graduate students are seeking information in localities for theses, more and more people in general are using local historical resources. Will one group know what the other is doing or what its members are talking about? To help bridge this gap, some introspection on the part of local historians, about what they are doing and about the nature of local history, is necessary.

My purpose in this volume is to deal with the particular conditions under which a local historian labors and to raise some basic questions about historical method. I am interested in constraints on a local historian placed by documents, by society in general, by the particular local situation, and by the individual him- or herself. I will raise questions about various aspects of a local historian's activities: the use of evidence, structure of research programs, language, relations with peers, problems of audience expectations, and publication. This discussion is not only important for local historians; it is essential that it also occur in historical agencies when exhibits or new publications are considered.

My intention is not to tell anyone how to write local history, set up an exhibit, or put together an impeccable footnote, because books and pamphlets on those topics already exist.[6] Rather, I intend to identify problems that are particular to the field of local history and to open discussion of them. If local historians and those who run historical agencies recognize the complexities inherent in their work—if they, if we, appreciate the reasons for the existence of those problems—we will become better, more thoughtful, historians. I have a great many questions to raise and situations to sketch out; I have few hard and fast answers—although when I do, I tend to present them as though they were handed down by Clio herself. I have neither all the answers nor even all the questions.

Such a discussion for local historians has been attempted only infrequently. In 1943, John Caughey identified some occupational hazards faced by local historians—although by "local," Caughey really meant people interested in state history rather than researchers involved with the history of their own communities.[7] Originally presented as a talk before the Pacific Coast Branch of the American Historical Association, Caughey's essay appeared in *The Pacific Historical Review*. In 1967, H. P. R. Finberg, tongue in cheek, noted some sins commonly committed by local historians in a sprightly essay entitled "How Not to Write a Local History," which also originated as a lecture and was then published in a volume of essays.[8] I have borrowed freely from both articles, although neither man is an amateur local historian. Both are now retired professors of history, the former from the University of California at Los Angeles, the latter from Leicester University, where he occupied the Chair of English Local History. While each identifies important issues, both neglect the beat and rhythm of a local historian's experience. Neither scholar views problems from the vantage of an amateur who keeps his or her own community's past. Others too, more recently, have written about local history; they have been consulted and will be mentioned in the course of these essays.

Conditions differ in our field from state to state and from one area to another. Some local historians are aided in their work by active state historical societies that provide information and advice to individuals involved in local history. In other places, historians have banded together locally to talk about their activities and to learn from each other—often under the aegis of the state historical society. In many states, local history activities are carefully considered, while in other states, local history and local historians receive little encouragement and consideration. Some local historians work alone. There is no way to speak to every situation. Because I work in the local history of my county, and of my portion of New York state, many of the illustrations in this book are drawn from close to home. Although I have read widely in preparation for this book, and in order to know what is current in many places, there is no way that I can be familiar with the specifics of local history in every place in the nation. I believe, however, that the situations and conditions discussed here are representative of problems faced by local historians everywhere, even if the specifics differ from place to place. If circumstances discussed here seem unduly old-fashioned or musty, you ought to feel grateful; if what is depicted here is comparable to the situation you know, you might take comfort in the knowledge that other historians are struggling to solve some of the same problems. I do not believe we suffer more gracefully if we know that others confront the same difficulties; but I do think that we can learn from the experiences of others to improve our own working conditions. That is really what these essays are all about.

I have tried to formulate questions about the local historian's experience, to suggest areas where problems lurk, and to warn of frequently encountered pitfalls and common failings. I hope to stimulate discussion about the issues, not to dictate answers or propose rigid formulas. I do not intend, in citing specific examples, to disparage amateur local historians—for I am one myself—but to suggest how very easy it is to fall into bad habits. My goal is not to point an accusing finger but to point at ways that the practice of local history in the United States might be improved by those of us who so happily occupy our time with it.

さぶう

A number of people have helped me with this book, and with the practice of local history over the past twenty years. They are, in some cases, people who have answered questions by mail or those who have talked to me on the telephone. Robert J. Smith, professor of anthropology at Cornell, has shared his extensive knowledge of Japan with me; Herbert Finch, Gould Colman, Nancy Dean, and Kathleen Jacklin at Cornell University Library have always been willing to talk with me; Stephen Bielinski and Paul Scudiere, of the State Department of Anthropological and Historical Services, in Albany, New York, have listened to my concerns and have frequently asked me to speak at meetings and seminars for local historians. Some of those who have helped have written local histories or worked in historical societies; I have always learned from the students I have set out to teach and from others who have written about the field. No individual alone knows enough; we rely upon and learn from others, and their contribution to our learning is important.

Two individuals in particular have always been candid, willing to read what I have written and to offer suggestions. One is my husband, Michael, whose contributions to the field of local history are not inconsiderable, even while he has taught and written about our past from a national perspective. The other is Wendell Tripp, editor of *New York History,* who has shared my concern for local history and who provided me an opportunity to write about local history for its practitioners in my own state. In addition, I am exceedingly grateful to Betty Doak Elder, former director of the AASLH Press, for encouraging me to write this book, to Judith Austin, who copyedited the manuscript, and to Gerald George, director of the American Association for State and Local History.

*Above Cayuga's waters*                                    CAROL KAMMEN
*Ithaca, New York*
*1986*

# NOTES

1. *The Local Historian* is issued four times a year for the British Association for Local History by the National Council for Voluntary Organizations, 26 Bedford Square, London, WC1B H3U, England.

2. Jacob Burckhardt, *Reflections on History* (Indianapolis, Indiana: Liberty Classics, 1979), 53-54; and Edward Shils, "On the Spirit and Form of Our Intellectual Institutions," *Bulletin of the American Academy of Arts and Sciences* 40 (April 1982): 9.

3. In response to the needs of historians who function outside the academy, *The Public Historian* was founded in the fall of 1978. This journal represents historians working in a variety of settings. It is published by the Graduate Program in Public Historical Studies, Department of History, University of California, Santa Barbara. Its editor is G. Wesley Johnson, Jr. Submissions are sought from "academic historians, public historians and other persons actively involved or concerned with historical research and interpretation in the community, government and private sectors." Manuscripts for *The Public Historian* may deal with various aspects of public history: commentaries that discuss and analyze various issues, methodologies, and professional matters pertaining to the field of public history and the work of public historians; research that uses historical methodology and perspective on matters concerning or benefiting community, government, and private sectors; reports describing the specific work and occupation of a public historian or others performing historical research in the community, government, and private sectors.

4. Editor, "Soapbox," in *CHAT* (County Historians [of New York] Association Tidings), (Rochester, New York), Summer, 1978.

5. "From Readers," *The Local Historian* 9 (February 1971): 226-232.

6. Thomas Felt, *Researching, Writing, and Publishing Local History* (Nashville: American Association for State and Local History, 1976); and Donald Dean Parker, *Local History, How to Gather It, Write It, and Publish It* (New York: Social Science Research Council, 1944).

7. *Pacific Historical Review* 12 (March 1943): 1-9.

8. H. P. R. Finberg, "Local History," in Finberg and V. H. T. Skipp, *Local History: Objective and Pursuit* (Newton Abbott, England: David and Charles, 1967), 71-86.

# 1 🐛 *Local History and Local Historians*

*Local history is not only a challenge to the most highly trained master of historical techniques; it is also — and long may it remain! — the last refuge of the non-specialist.*

H. P. R. FINBERG (1962)[1]

LOCAL HISTORY has long been with us, practiced in many cultures for many different purposes. Local history is sometimes clouded in myth, colored by forms of ancestor worship, or confused with ideas of patriotism or boosterism. It can be dated to the sixteenth century in England and to approximately the same period in France. In both countries, it grew out of interest in nobility, castles, coinage, parishes, armorial bearings, and lineages. Some of the books produced were well done, if limited in outlook, while others were "mere vestiges of error, and some of fraud, which time and vanity had rendered sacred."[2] Most were written without any plan or thesis, and whatever information was known about an area was included.

The pattern of writing history in the New World is little different from that in the Old. Writing history in the colonial period was often stimulated by political motives, while some history was providential, "proving" God's will and America's unique mission. In the eighteenth century, history writing in the colonies tended to be colored by political points of view. Books stressed a provincial identity, often with an eye to encouraging immigration. After the American Revolution, history writing tended to justify the actions of Americans in the recent war, and it attempted to create a national myth. While there were local histories right from the start in the eastern states, most attempts at writing the history of a particular community date from the 1840s for a good part of the nation, and after the Centennial in 1876 for just about every other place that was substantially settled by then. Hermann E. Ludewig, writing in 1846, noted: "No people in the world can have so great an interest in the history of their country, as that of the U.S. of North America: for there are none who enjoy an equally great share in their country's historical acts." He insisted that the history of the United States contains the "political and moral history of mankind, and it points to the way of greater perfection, which a free nation ought continually to strive to attain."[3]

By and large, local histories written prior to 1870 were written by persons called by one scholar "patrician historians."[4] "Patrician" might aptly describe some of these writers, but many others among our nineteenth-century authors might better be called members of the nascent professional classes whose occupations allowed them the leisure to engage in the writing of history. What these men — and they *were* nearly all men — had in common was some measure of education and an interest in writing elegant pieces about their hometowns. These newspaper publishers, editors, lawyers, doctors, and ministers who wrote much of the earlier nineteenth-century local history had some common concerns, and because they generally created the first — sometimes the only — history of a community, their attitudes toward history writing have come down to us today. Their style of writing has influenced the public's idea of what local history is and how it should be presented, and they created the patterns from which many local historians have yet to be emancipated.

These writers hoped to lure settlers into their areas. They promoted the healthy situation of their towns or counties. Many of their histories were commemorative, a memorial or a remembrance of the early settlers. H. C. Goodwin, in his book of history, wrote that

it is a duty which we of the present generation owe to the memory of the pioneers of civilization in the region of the country where we dwell, to gather up with care whatever records of the times there are left, and studying them well, transmit them in the most enduring form to successive ages.

If Goodwin wrote because of a duty that the present owed to the past, Franklin B. Hough wrote because "there are certain duties which the Present owes to the Future, to transmit in a permanent form the record of the Past, that the memory of olden time, and the names of those who have aided in the formation of society fall not into oblivion. . . ."[5]

Some local histories were written to show the degree of culture to be found in an area, so that a community would not be written off as backward or regarded by its residents (or others) as a backwater. To this end, a number of authors produced pamphlets in the guise of history. "The contrast," wrote one author in 1847, extolling the present state of a village as compared with its rude beginnings some fifty years earlier,

is hardly to be comprehended. The change from toil, privation, and constant efforts to those of ease, repose, and tranquility; from the hardy pioneer's life, to one of affluence and splendor; from the rustic garb to the finer and most costly fabrics of American and English manufacture; from a dense wilderness, to rich, fertile fields; from low, filthy, and miasmatic lagoons, to dry, healthy, and beautiful flower gardens; from the absence of learning and literary pursuit, to the flooding of every species of intelligence.[6]

Progress was, in this case, change that had improved life and eased toil. Change tended to be viewed as more ominous, however, when it brought about alterations in the character of the population or the mores of a community. Progress could mean increase, from little to fulfillment; for those who worked hard, it was the deserved and expected reward. Later changes were seen as destructive of old values when they created diversity of population or altered leadership patterns from people who had traditionally held power and influence to newcomers.

The Fourth of July was an occasion when history was sometimes expounded in an oral presentation. When public lectures became the vogue in our small communities, the history of a town was considered a fitting topic. These orations frequently treated events as if chronology alone were enough, yet the public found such annals acceptable, and they tended when published to be popular souvenirs.[7]

Some histories were imitative, or were a form of competition, written because another community (particularly a neighbor) already had such a record. "That which suggested the present enterprise and which has resulted in the production of the following history," noted one author in 1840, was the reading of another town's book.[8] He then asserted that such a work "would not be without interest *even* to the present generation." This last statement reveals another important motivation for the writing of local history: such histories were often regarded as inspirational and instructional, especially to the youth of a community—young people who took for granted and were perhaps even becoming discontented with the places in which they lived. The unrelenting story in these "small histories" is of a hardy pioneer who moved to virgin land and, by dint of hard work and belief in the Christian religion, made for himself and his family the rosy existence that they presently enjoyed. The hardy pioneer's wife is rarely mentioned, but that is another problem altogether. These histories present a didactic lesson, even to the contemporary generation, and "cannot fail to be deeply interesting and instructive to the present inhabitants."[9]

Some histories, like newspapers of the era, were forms of local boosterism, demonstrating that a small enclave was the center of all that was progressive and enterprising. In fact, these two words recur over and over again in the descriptions of places about which our local historians wrote. They were reflecting, of course, words that the settling generation used: the first steamboat on Cayuga Lake was called *The Enterprise.* Comparable examples abound.

These histories promoted a town, boosted its image, and attempted to demonstrate—especially to youth—that prosperity can be found at home. They also played upon feelings of local pride and clannish associations. "Those who read this volume," stated one historian, "will find their fathers or ancestors, their relations or acquaintance," for the book was about the land of their nativity—or perhaps of their adoption. Such sentiments were important to cultivate, the same writer noted, "because it is upon the love of family and country, that all the social and virtuous affections are based." Ultimately, these histories were a form of filiopietism or ancestor worship, of patriotism and attachment to the particular place where one belonged.[10]

George Callcott, writing in 1970, claimed that the pre-Civil War interest in local history "has never since been equaled." He also noted that "the more geographically limited the interest of historians were, the more modest their accomplishments" and that town histories were written by a lot of "generally poor historians." Those histories with a broader geographic base, he claimed, tend to have had a more lasting impact; for example, Timothy Flint's and John Wesley Monette's histories of the Mississippi Valley and Henry Howe's historical collections of the West were more important than town chronicles that were "generally detailed, highly factual, liberally sprinkled with genealogy, and frequently 700 pages or more in length."[11] To a community, however, the town chronicles survived and were cherished, a fact that Callcott overlooked.

Local histories were often written to promote local and national heroes. Indeed, they mention the major figures in a town's past, and certainly every "important figure" who passed through the area is given his due. These histories do more than promote public heroes, though. They tend to democratize the possibility of heroism: that is, to see heroism in Everyman, or at least in every citizen of the community (excluding, of course, blacks, transients, women, and people whose position was marginal). Each settler mentioned in local history was one who started anew, and each built a satisfactory life for himself and his family. Those who did not succeed, or did not remain on the land, were omitted from the history; while those who stayed in the community and appeared upstanding, strove for material success, earthly rewards, and a Christian afterlife, were seen in heroic or at least historic proportions. The success of the early settlers, said one author, "induced many to look with desire toward this county." Where history in Europe concentrated on the church and the manor, local history in the United States extolled the successful business-

man, the manufacturer, and especially the hardworking farmer. If
this sounds rather like Thomas Jefferson's yeoman farmer, the back-
bone of a republican society, it is no accident.[12]

Jefferson's views were surely known to the writers of our local histories, but so were the opinions, and the styles of writing, and the
literary conventions of classical historians. Many educated American
males — the patrician or leisured historians — knew Latin and Greek
or read the ancients in translation; in the examples in their histories
and in the language patterns in which they wrote, we can hear the
ancients echo through our own American setting.

Washington Irving laid out his debt, and his knowledge of the
ancient historical tradition, in his *Knickerbocker History.* He stated
that like Herodotus, who lacked written records, he endeavored to
"continue the chain of history by well authenticated traditions"; that
like Xenophon, he maintained the utmost impartiality and the strict-
est adherence to truth; as in the manner of Sallust, he enriched
his history with portraits of "ancient worthies," drawn at full length
and faithfully colored. Thucydides had taught him to season his history with political speculations; but as did Tacitus, Irving sweetened
it with the "graces of sentiment" and infused the whole with the
"dignity, grandeur and magnificence of Livy." Finally, he had, like
Polybius, sought to make out of the disparate facts that came to hand
a history that had unity.[13] Washington Irving's history of Manhattan
is satirical in tone, intended to amuse the public and to sell books.
It was a literary *tour de force,* written pen in cheek. Most other local
historians took themselves and their histories rather more seriously.

Local history became popular in the Centennial Era in part
because President Ulysses S. Grant called upon Americans to write
the history of their localities; the nation was seen as the sum of its
parts. Literacy was on the rise, and for some people there was increased
leisure and a great interest in self-improvement, one route to which
was seen as history.

While the nation's Centennial in 1876 contributed to the explosion of interest in the writing of local history, other things, too, caused
interest in the field. John Higham has pointed out that during the

nineteenth century "the study of history in various forms . . . superseded the study of the classics as the chief vehicle for enabling man to know himself."[14] This shift from the classics to history can be seen throughout the century. One writer of local history noted that there are two sources of information, philosophy and history. The former addresses itself to understanding, while history enhances understanding and the imagination, and wakens the sympathies of the heart. Of the two, history is the more important. Having minimized philosophy, the author looks more closely at history and poses a new dilemma for himself. He recognizes the study of antiquity as the greatest subject of history. How can he then reconcile the values of antiquity with the fact that the work he is presenting to the public is one of American local history—a subject barely two generations old? Easily done, smiles our clever author: The antiquity of the world is the story of its creation and of the people of ancient civilizations. So, too, the antiquity of the author's section of America is told as the story of its era of settlement and of the valiant pioneers who struggled to make it home. Although that settlement took place only fifty years earlier, he argued, it still had all the charm "as it would have if it had taken [place] five hundred years ago!"[15]

There are some less attractive reasons, too, why people turned to local history in this period. The last twenty years of the nineteenth century were a time of increased immigration to the United States by people whose ethnic diversity challenged the hegemony of native-born Americans; a time when class divisions became apparent, when political disillusionment, fear of the unruly, and labor unrest swept the nation. Few of these aspects of the era were treated by the local historical societies being formed everywhere, for those associations became the refuge for people who felt beleaguered by change and who feared that their way of life would not survive the onslaught. So local histories recalled old times; they chronicled the genesis of a community, its first settlers, its prominent citizens, and the values that they shared. Local histories presented a history of steady progression from rude beginnings to a contemporary civilized state, with home, family, patriotism, hard work, and Christianity brought along intact, "to illustrate the privations, virtues, piety, patriotism, and enterprise of her people," states one history of a New York community. All the while, the treatment accorded to the pioneers of a community became a sanctified litany, a legacy that remains with us today.[16]

Other motives stated by writers of local histories near the end of the nineteenth century included a desire to "rescue materials from fast-gathering oblivion" and a concern to collect the memories of older persons who could themselves tell, or who could remember stories told to them, of the earliest days of the community. Some writers wanted to "correct many errors" in past historical accounts and to "correctly narrate these important historical events."[17]

Gilbert W. Hazeltine's preface to his *Early History of the Town of Ellicott,* in Chatauqua County, New York, sums up the motivations and style of many of these nineteenth-century gentleman writers. Hazeltine was a local doctor, and his preface, while lengthy, is so exemplary that it deserves our attention.

What is the *ratio justifica* of this book? Simply this. *Our friends desired us to write it, and we wrote it;* the Journal Printing Company printed it, and Merz put on the covers. It is a home made book for home use; and the critics, if any, we expect to be to the manor born.

Our friends will justify themselves by saying,—"we desired to rescue the memory of our grandfathers and our grandmothers, and our parents, from the deep pall of oblivion which was fast settling down upon them,—and the history of their homes in the wilderness, in which they labored so hard to secure blessings which we alone have lived to reap and to enjoy. The hardy, generous, and in many instances gifted men and women, who lived and labored in what are now our busy streets, have left enduring monuments of their united labor, but the records of their individual selves, have been meagre and unsatisfactory. The records imprinted on the memories of a few yet living—whose boyhood days were spent in Jamestown, before it had become an incorporated village, have been found, of all remaining sources of information, the most reliable and satisfactory. There are still living here a number of persons who became citizens from 1825 to 1835, whose memory of events has yielded material assistance by sustaining and strengthening the memory of the writer,—by what they themselves knew of, and had frequently heard related, of the early settlers. As the years roll on, their deeds would soon have been forgotten, if the extended sketches we have caused to be made by one who was an onlooker, had not been written and given to the world." This is the answer you elicit from our friends.

It has been our attempt to record the names and the deeds of the fathers, surrounded by all that constituted their homes — as we once saw them, and as, to-day, they are vividly depicted in our memory. We have labored to place before you, their children and successors — pictures of their persons,— their homes,— and their surroundings in the long ago when Jamestown was a hamlet in the wilderness — when the Pearl City was the Rapids — when instead of the busy *hum* of a hundred factories and a thousand industries, and a city of comfortable homes and palace residences there were a few lowly dwellings, and the hum was of the saw mill and the busy boatman by day, and the howl of the wolf or the scream of the wild cat in the Big Fly, by night. The homes, the industries, the scenes here depicted, were to our noble but humble-minded fathers the all of human life — they bounded the horizon of their being — they were the environments of their existence. Memory had embalmed them in the hearts of their children, now few remaining, old and fast passing away. What is known of these Pioneers among the children's children, the present generation, is weak and shadowy, and is yearly becoming more and more dim, and at the end of another decade — even within that short period — *folk lore* would have claimed the little remaining of the memory of the early settlers. We interpose this feeble book to prevent such a disaster. We present it as a rough monument to their memories — their homes — their deeds — their lives.

Although conscious that we have used every effort, which could be reasonably expected, to accurately describe the scenes and events herein depicted, yet the invariable experience of others should teach us not to claim entire exemption from those errors and imperfections always found in works of biography and history. History has been defined [as] "An approximation towards truth." We cannot believe that this definition even *approximates* to a true one — nevertheless it may *embody a shadow* of a truth, for every thing human is marked by imperfections.[18]

🐟

In the 1880s, history emerged as a profession throughout the United States, and gentleman historians yielded to university professors for whom historical activity was not an avocation, but a specialized career. These men made history an institutional product. David Van Tassel ends his book on the origins of history writing in the United States with the epitaph that by 1884 "the long age of the amateur historian had ended."[19] Yet during this era, when departments of history were being instituted in American universities and young men were looking seriously at historical studies as a career, amateur local historians were not spurned. There was no intention, at the outset, to make a division between the two groups.

Quite the contrary. One of the most influential practitioners of history, and a founder of the American Historical Association, set out in a very different direction. Herbert Baxter Adams went to Johns Hopkins University when that institution opened in 1876, after having studied for a Ph.D. in Heidelberg, Germany. Adams had the title of Fellow at Johns Hopkins, and he soon began teaching a graduate seminar in history. He directed his history students to local topics while he himself prepared a paper on the role that Maryland's delegates had played in the Continental Congress — a paper that he delivered at a meeting of the Maryland Historical Society. Adams attempted to promote cooperation between "the local cultural establishment and the emerging professoriat."[20] He particularly stressed the importance of publishing colonial documents, and he urged the state to provide funds so that those materials might be made available.

At the same time that Adams was promoting local studies, Charles Kendall Adams, president of Cornell University, suggested that a professional historical society be formed. Herbert Baxter Adams took the idea forward, and he shepherded the American Historical Association into being. It was his intention that the new association include gentleman scholars as well as professionals and that the AHA would also provide direction for local historical societies. "The implicit theory of the association was that the professors would lead and yet welcome and honor outstanding amateur historians and seek to coordinate efforts of the many local historical societies."[21]

It did not work out so smoothly, however, for the needs of the professionals and the amateurs did not dovetail well. One young professor complained in 1889: "There were more nobs than usual in attendance . . . I am a little inclined to think the thing is getting into the hands of elderly swells who dabble in history."[22] But the amateurs had their complaints, too. Edward Eggleston wrote that same year that the American Historical Association "seems to be run in the interest of college professors only and to give those of us who are not of that clan the cold shoulder." With some exceptions, the amateurs gradually drifted away. In 1904, a Conference of State and Local Historical Societies was created, meeting in conjunction with the AHA but arranging its own program and agenda.[23]

The amateur historian was certainly eclipsed, during these last years of the nineteenth century and in the early days of the twentieth, but by no means did the amateur disappear—a fact ignored in most of the literature concerning the development of historical writing in the United States. Rather, the amateur persisted, and some continued to write very fine books indeed: Theodore Roosevelt, an accomplished amateur historian, was even made president of the American Historical Association, and Franklin D. Roosevelt, as town historian, wrote a history of Hyde Park, New York. Amateurs continued the work of collecting, preserving, and writing local history. While academic historians tackled national issues, they tended to overlook the history of America's hometowns. Throughout the country, local historical societies proliferated and pursued the collecting of documents and artifacts, and local historians produced local studies. Learning from the academics, these local historians hoped their work would be more complete and more accurate than previously written local history and that they could rescue information apt otherwise to be lost or destroyed. However, these later authors also admitted to a degree of censorship of topics included in their histories, in order—like their predecessors—to present a community's past in the most favorable light. One writer stressed that he wrote of those events worthy of preservation, while another wanted to produce a history "of which all citizens can be proud."[24]

During this era, other occupations professionalized, and the practitioners of local history began to change. Many of the patrician historians—our middle-class gentlemen of some education and local status—removed themselves from the writing of local history. The newcomers who moved into the field quickly demonstrated that the challenge presented by local history was difficult for them and that they were unaccustomed to the task of writing. One author, Christfield Johnson, who wrote a centennial history of Erie County, New York, noted that his book had taken him fifteen months of continuous work. "Had I known," he wrote, "the amount of labor involved, and the very poor pay to be obtained, it is doubtful whether I should have attempted the task." He also said: "If any one thinks it easy to harmonize and arrange the immense number of facts and dates here treated of, let him try to learn the precise circumstances regarding a single event, occuring twenty years ago, and he will soon find how widely authorities differ."[25]

Another author stated that his history had taken a quarter of a century to research and write. A third man complained that he had spent fourteen months writing his history. "I have been much puzzled," he wrote, "as to what to leave out. My promise was to make a book of 480 pages," but the book he completed required well over 800. Arad Thomas protested that he was "not a professional book maker and has no hope of founding a literary reputation on this work." These complaints were never voiced by the writers of earlier histories, who had had the education to be comfortable with the task of writing and who, with some surety, picked their way through the tangle of information.[26]

The most significant stimuli to writers of local history at the end of the nineteenth century were the commercial publishers who hired authors to produce local histories. They believed that there was a substantial market for local history, despite the narrow geographical area involved, and these publishers counted on people being willing to pay to have a book containing the names and deeds of family and friends. The publishers devised a way of meeting their costs before they ever had books to offer for sale, and they thereby faced little financial risk. Throughout the East there were a number of companies who kept their presses busy by turning out city and county histories. The books offered to the public were fat volumes, full of information and profusely illustrated. These books were not really written, but rather compiled by agents of the publishing company with the aid of people in the community. Nor were these books really narrative history; but they were compilations of historical sketches, containing a great deal of historical information.

If we look at the example of D. Mason and Company, of Syracuse, New York, we can begin to understand the scale of this new undertaking. Mason and Company published seven New York county histories in seven years, all the while involved with large histories of counties in Ohio and Pennsylvania. In 1884, for example, Mason hired H. P. Smith to compile a history of Buffalo and Erie County. The next year, Smith put together a history of Cortland County, plus a volume on Broome County. Then he moved on. Smith commented:

it is the general plan of the publishers in the production of county histories to secure, as far as possible, local assistance in preparing the work, either as writers, or for the purpose of revising all manuscripts; the consequence being that the work bears a local character that could not otherwise be secured, and moreover, comes from the press far more complete and perfect than could possibly be the case were it entrusted entirely to the hands of a comparative stranger to the locality treated of.[27]

Neither Smith nor any of the other compilers who were hired to put together a history could possibly have written the story of a county in six months. A compiler would place a notice in a local newspaper to announce his intended project, and then he would visit prominent people in the community to solicit their help. He gathered information, invited industries or individuals and local institutions to write blurbs or donate material about themselves for inclusion, and offered them the opportunity to place their pictures in the book. Harold Nestler, who has studied and collected county histories for some time, cites the case of a man who paid W. W. Munsell and Company, an Albany publisher, $150 to have his portrait and biography included in a county history. The subscriber received one copy of the book and twenty extra copies of the photograph. The going rate for such inclusions ranged from $50 to $300 an entry, and in this way the company recovered the cost of the book well ahead of its publication.[28]

Publishers advertised that the biographies included in county histories were representative of men of all professions: that is, that local history was eclectic, not elitist. In these books, we find portraits and biographies of upstanding farmers and businessmen, lawyers, self-made men, and descendants of early pioneer families that had come into the area with little and built comfortable lives for themselves. If each picture included in a county history cost $50, the lowest amount mentioned, the publishers of an average book, with 96 images, could net $4,800 prior to publication. If, on the other hand, the average of the various forms of inclusion from small portraits to a double-page spread showing house, barn, animals, and inset portraits was $100, the publishers could amass, prior to the sales of the book, somewhere in the neighborhood of $9,600. This sum is enough to pay for publication of a book today, although not one quite so profusely illustrated. Imagine the profits realized one hundred years ago!

Why did people want to be included in such a volume, and at rates that can only be considered steep? What did inclusion in a county history mean to people who paid $100, $150, or more for the privilege? Obviously one thing these people achieved was a form of immortality, establishing themselves as solid, upstanding citizens, able to buy their way into such a book if they desired. Thus the farmer with $150 to spend distanced himself from those who were simply eking out an existence on the soil, or from those who had just arrived in the area and had no means to pay for space in such a book and little stake in the community. The businessman, too, was able to show his worth, display his lineage, and purchase a form of everlasting advertising.

The history offered in these publishers' ventures was standardized fare, as the tables of contents in the commercial local histories testify. They were virtually interchangeable, and the biographical inclusions, whether the subject lived in Suffolk or in St. Louis, were treated much alike.

Richard Dorson, the Indiana folklorist, pointed out that county histories from the northeast part of the nation

told one rigid, undeviating story. They began with a reference to Indians and the wilderness topography; hailed the first settlers, noted the first churches; the first schools, the first stores; devoted a chapter to the Revolution and the local patriots; swung into full stride with the establishment of the newspaper, the militia, the fire department, and the waterworks; rhapsodized about the fraternal lodges and civic organizations; recounted the prominent citizens of the community, and enumerated famous personages (chiefly Washington and Lafayette) who had passed through; listed a roster of the Civil War dead; and rounded off the saga with descriptions of the newest edifices on Main Street.[29]

The title of Washington Frothingham's history says it all. His book was called *History of Montgomery County* [New York] *Embracing Early Discoveries; the Advance of Civilization; The Labors and Triumphs of Sir William Johnson; The Inception of Development of Manufacturers; With Town and Local Records; Also Military Achievements of Montgomery Patriots.* This, Frothingham promised, was a history "of which all citizens could be proud."[30]

The second new group who moved into the world of the patrician historian consisted of women. In 1883, the Association of Collegiate Alumnae suggested avenues of activity other than teaching appropriate for women, and local history was included among them. Prior to the 1880s, there were few local histories written by women. In New York state, of all the nineteenth-century histories surveyed, I have found only two written by women. From the 1880s onward, although slowly at first, women could be found involving themselves with local history until eventually they became its primary keepers. It has been estimated that of New York's 1600 local historians who today are listed by the State Department of Education, 80 percent are women, and most of them are over the age of fifty-five.[31]

When women enter a field, be it teaching or typewriting, a devaluation of prestige and monetary return often follows. There was never much—if any—money to be made by local historians, and the presence of great numbers of women probably assured that there never would be; local history could never derive esteem from the money it generated. Its regard came because of the connection local history made with place, with "old times and values," and because of the local status of its early practitioners. As most editors, publishers, and lawyers eased out of the field, the rising prestige of their own professions left with them — leaving commercial publishers, with their compilers, and women. Thus in the early years of the twentieth century, local history underwent something of a decline in prestige: feminized and commercialized. In addition, the errors of its past caused the public to regard it with less favor. Russel Headley, whose own work promised to "hue [sic] straight to the line," wrote in 1908:

It is a well-known fact that considerable prejudice exists among a great body of the people toward county histories in general, for the reason that some such compilations in the past, have been composed of fact and fiction so intermingled, as to render it a difficult matter to know what was true and what was false.[32]

Other significant factors were also at work to accelerate this decline of interest in local history. America was undergoing rapid change. The automobile altered transportation patterns and much, much more. World War I opened to Americans a vision of a life beyond the ocean; the 1920s roared for change and mocked the tyranny and mustiness of the past. Nothing could have been more old-fashioned, more passe, more out of date than local history. Malcolm Cowley complained in his memoir that education in his youth (ca. 1916) was aimed at "destroying whatever roots we had in the soil, toward eradicating our local and regional peculiarities, toward making us homeless citizens." Cowley believed that only Southerners retained any sense of place. "We were divested of our pride," for students, he noted, studied every history but that of where they were — a prejudice, he insisted, that existed in public schools and in universities alike. George Callcott noted, on the question of teaching local history, that "the subject of local history was never really popular in the schools despite state loyalty and even state laws."[33]

As widespread popular interest in local history dwindled, most commercial publishers withdrew from the field. Getting local history published thereafter became a more difficult task. Historical societies sometimes picked up the cost, but more often an author paid for the publication of his or her own book. These were expedients, however, the former perhaps more acceptable than the latter. As one indication of this trend, J. Franklin Jameson wrote James Truslow Adams about a woman from central New York who had written him asking how to go about having a book of local history published. Adams was at a loss for an answer: his own first book had been privately printed, while his second, a history of Southampton, New York, was "brought out for his own profit by the local printer who had printed the first one." Adams cautioned that the locale of the history might make a book more commercially acceptable: if, he suggested, the community is like Concord, Massachusetts, with an interest in history and a built-in tourist trade, the book might do well, and a publisher might be found. For a less historic place, he had slim hopes.[34]

At this point we find yet another type of individual interested in local history. Printers, pressmen, town clerks, and postal carriers, during the 1920s and 1930s, began to put their names on books and pamphlets of local history. I cannot document this trend with absolute numbers, but I have collected the names and biographies of several of these individuals and have indications of others. One was Uri Mulford, who published in 1920 lists of marriages, births, deaths, and past events as a history of Corning, New York. In the introduction to this book, Mulford, whose education and position in society were far from those held by our patrician historians of the previous century, stated boldly:

This book was written, the type set, the pages made ready for the press, and the printing done on his own press, by Uri Mulford. If I had not devoted a great deal of time during nearly a score of years, to research work, and had not purchased the printing equipment necessary to produce these pages, this unique, authentic and comprehensive history, *Pioneer Days and Later Times in Corning and Vicinity* could not by any possibility have been produced. The cost of production would have been prohibitive. The major factor in the success of the project, however, was my skill as a master printer — a craft that I have followed with minor periods of interruption for a full half-century.[35]

Another among this group of pressmen believed that footnotes impeded or intimidated the ordinary reader and refused to allow them in the pamphlets he produced. He wanted to entertain the public by using the materials of local history. He cared very much that people know about the history of the place where they lived, and he believed that it mattered not a whit if the stories were historically accurate or could be traced through scholarly apparatus. Another member of this group, when asked why he chased down bits of the past, replied that he was interested in preserving little items about common people "for Posterity."

Does it really matter? asked the reporter interviewing him.

He "looked genuinely surprised. He was silent for a moment, peering over his gold-rim glasses. 'Don't you think other people will enjoy it?' "[36]

Professional historians did not completely ignore local history. From time to time, the American Historical Association studied the issue of local history and debated the association's responsibility for and relationship to it. At its 1914 meeting, a committee of the Mississippi Valley Historical Association offered seven reasons why state universities should offer courses in state or local history. It was a state university's obligation to advance learning and promote culture; states owed something to history and were under obligation to preserve their own; courses in state and local history were more appropriate for graduate than for undergraduate students because "other things than state and local history are more likely to be conducive to a student's culture, to his training, to his higher education." In addition, a state university should be ready and willing to lend aid and cooperation to the agencies within the state for promotion of public interest and knowledge concerning state history; the university should collect and publish materials pertaining to state history, and these activities should be under the auspices of departments of history; and — last but not least — research in state and local history was a rich field for graduate students as an exercise in how to do history, and local studies could be useful to national historians.[37]

A representative to the meeting from the University of North Dakota dissented. He noted that in many states, university people and historical society people did not come in contact: "in outer darkness are the people interested in state history." He also noted that professors of history would have to learn how to deal with people who carry history around in their heads, either as participants or as descendants. A professor would have to learn how to interview "to obtain valuable historical information," and professors would need to understand that "the folks will haze him if possible as being an easy mark." He did note that state history would guarantee a writer a large audience, although those most interested would be "the pioneers of the state," and probably not any others. The role of graduate students would be to gain access for the professor "to the people."[38]

❧

During the twentieth century, local history acquired one of its most popular forms. Newspaper writers of the 1930s—and continuing to this day—seized upon local history as interesting material for feature articles and for weekly columns. Local history had appeared in newspapers before, of course, but mostly in the form of reminiscences, letters, and sometimes the results of interviews with aged or notable people. On occasion, a newspaper would publish a document that had surfaced, and of course newspapers noted the anniversaries of town foundings, community institutions, and disasters.

The appearance of local history in the 1930s took a slightly new form, however. Journalists who reveled in an anecdote, or a joke, or regional dialect would take a story, polish it, and present it to the paper's readers. Their interest was in the telling of highly specific stories, which they did with verve. The demands that these journalists faced included the needs of editors to fill space with local, particular, "upbeat," hometown material; the pressures of deadline; and the desire to amuse or entertain readers. Ultimately, these writers were trying to sell newspapers and maintain reader loyalty. Such newspaper writers were and continue to be very influential. They told pieces of a community's past in its most readily available form and in an entertaining fashion. Some of their stories are insightful — important additions to an area's knowledge of its own past. The purpose of these writers was to take local history out of the hands of those who make it dull and wearisome, to democratize it, and eventually to commercialize it. As one of these journalists wrote: "But what about the self-trumpeted historians who are determined to keep history for the few by locking it up except on appointed occasions or deliberately making it dull?" He stormed on: "A few of us are trying to make . . . history more alive than it was made for us." When asked whether his work was fact or fiction, he said he didn't care a whit so long as it was read.[39]

These newspaper writers were determined to inject some vitality into history, and they did. Their newspaper columns were popular then, and they continue to be. Not only did the public get a snappy story to accompany the news and sports, they also acquired a notion of what local history could and should be. Local history was considered a source of local entertainment, as well as a source of local pride. [See chapter five, "Writing Local History in the Popular Press," pages 149-166.]

The ways of doing local history in the past have been as varied as the reasons for writing local history. Older histories established patterns that amateur historians and the public have accepted as suitable for the genre. W. G. Hoskins, an influential English historian, noted that "in trying to guide local historians into the paths of righteousness and away from the amateurish imbecilities that often marked much of their work in the past, I am in danger of taking all the pleasure out of local history."[40] To change the format is often to lose the very people for whom one is writing; the newspaper writers presenting history in the popular press are among the very few to attract a new category of readers.

While the topics deemed suitable for history have remained much the same through the years, the topics ignored by local historians have also remained constant. Local historians have been, on the whole, anti-modern; they have been overly concerned with beginnings and with the distribution of land. Local historians have rarely touched upon topics that concern change, especially alterations brought about by technology or the diversification of the population. As time has gone by, our local histories have repeated themselves—often to the point of reprinting earlier versions outright. The table of contents of a local history published in 1950 is like one of the 1850s, with a few new chapters added to account for the additional years. The outlook is similar from one century to the next, and the historical method used in 1850 is much the same as that used today. The motives of authors of local histories are similar, too, and local histories at mid-twentieth century reflect historical patterns of the previous century, with little regard to advances or changes in historical thinking and methodology.[41]

There have been some significant developments in the historical profession, however, and these are just now breaking in upon local historians, who cannot help but react to some of the forms that they take. An early inroad into local history by academic historians began in the 1930s with the development of a subdiscipline called "urban history." Moving away from political and economic history on a national scale, some professional historians embarked upon studies of America's urban centers. They looked at sources local historians had long used, and some others that local historians had neglected; and they produced studies that asked about change over time, that sought to identify the continuities that persisted despite a community's growth. Blake McKelvey's studies of Rochester are models of this genre. Constance McLaughlin Green, another urban historian, wrote as early as 1940 that history "from the bottom up" (her phrase) needed to look at various aspects of community life, to explain what happened (and where, and when) and also why. She complained that most of the local histories she had seen were written for community self-glorification, were antiquarian, lacked perspective, and were dull. She recommended that local historians study the field methods of the sociologist and read cultural anthropology in order to gain a broader understanding of history and historical methods. In 1940, Green called for studies of nondominant groups in a community, of class antagonisms, and of the emergence of social responsibility.[42] Such studies require careful use of historical documents, of course, and a respect for what emerges from them. Merle Curti commented that he saw the need

for cultural histories of communities: studies that would yield information about the backgrounds and education of settlers and later citizens; cleavages in communities and their various effects upon community institutions; the roles played by church, school, and press; the forces, too little studied, which differentiate one community from another; and the relations of Main Street to the world.

Curti also noted that "here the vigorous local interest that is sometimes channeled into antiquarian backwaters can join deep historical currents."[43]

The work of Green and Curti and other urban historians (whose important research continues to this day) has had relatively little impact upon local historians. One academic historian told me recently that only three copies of his important study of a community had been sold in that place. Local historians tend to continue in established patterns, their history rich with detail, quaint ways, and sayings, their readers content. In 1950, Richard Shryock noted that two types of historiography had developed in the United States. "The professionals," he wrote, "were concerned with over-all developments and interpretations; the local historians with a summary of the facts." He observed that local historians tended to be interested in "everything which had happened just because it had happened."[44]

An institutional linkage between local historians and the history professionals was formed with the birth, in 1940, of the American Association for State and Local History. That organization has advanced the cause of local history and its practitioners in a variety of ways. Today, the greatest potential bonds among the various workers in Clio's field are a new wave of interest in local historical studies on the part of academic historians and a new sense of purpose among local historians. The "new" social history has spread into many areas of academic historical work; its research materials are to be found in America's localities, and it has the potential to interest both groups of historians. Its researchers turn to local archives and to questions of a demographic nature in order to know the past more fully. New studies of mobility, religion, population, and family life have opened up new historical questions and exciting ways of seeking answers.[45]

This "new" social history did not spring into being without antecedents. They can be sought in the work of American urban historians and among historians abroad. In England, academic interest in local history in the later 1950s culminated with the Chair of English Local History, established at the University of Leicester. Interested in the origin, rise, and decline of communities, the Leicester School sought to encourage careful, thoughtful work by amateurs and professionals alike. Today, British social historians have expanded upon the outlook of the Leicester School and embarked upon broader demographic studies of English life in the past.[46]

In France, the route to local history came in the form of demographic studies rooted in department, or provincial, records. Researchers there sought the answers to questions of national importance in local archives. Local history alone, the great French historian Marc Bloch stated, "makes the study of more general problems possible." Wedded to this use of sources in villages and in department archives was the quest for knowledge concerning all of society, not merely information about those people who traditionally had power and about whom history had generally been written. This was history that built carefully from an economic understanding of village life to look at all the people in the area, their system of work, and ultimately their culture. In addition, French historians attempted to understand long-range trends in population changes — trends that were probably unperceived even by the participants themselves. These gigantic studies were ultimately made possible by limiting the area in which the researcher worked: that is, the geographic area of the study put reasonable limits on questions about the nature of life in the past. The computer became the technological assistant that made it possible to deal with such vast quantities of materials in new and sophisticated ways.[47]

In the United States, the "new" social history borrowed from these foreign trends and suited them to the types of information found in this country. During the 1970s and 1980s, there has been academic interest in local history, but that interest does not in any way account for local history's new popularity with the general public. In the 1970s, the country experienced *Roots*, the *Foxfire* series of books that focused on traditional life and folkways, and the preservation movement that touched so many of our cities and towns. In addition, the national celebration of the Bicentennial took place, in its most meaningful form, in America's hometowns. Just as during the period of the Centennial celebration in 1876, the Bicentennial stressed our hometown heritage, and with it came an outpouring of interest in local history. A new crop of books sprang up. Unfortunately, many were simply reprints of older, nineteenth-century histories, but some were new works of history written by local authors.

🐦

Now, too, almost one hundred years after the first appearance of commercial local histories, we are in the midst of an interesting revival of an idea whose time, it seems, has come once again. In some places, histories of our cities and counties are being written, commissioned by commercial publishing companies, just as they were in the 1880s. The idea of producing local histories may have begun during the Bicentennial with Continental Heritage Press of Tulsa, Oklahoma. Heritage hit upon a way to provide histories for large and medium-sized cities around the country by approaching local chambers of commerce and historical societies to discuss the availability of local corporate support for such books. Other companies followed suit. At first, a spokesman said, "Heritage thought that they had invented the wheel," only to be disappointed to find that it was an idea that had first seen the light of day one hundred years earlier.[48] The modern companies usually send an agent into a community to set up the financial sponsorship for a local history. A number of prepaid subscriptions for the book are required, and a quantity of pages must be pre-sold for commercial advertising at approximately $2,500 a page. For a volume about Binghamton, New York, Laurence Bothwell, county historian and co-author of the book, estimates that $100,000 or more was raised in that city from the business community before the book was even written. When financial arrangements have been settled, a local author is sought.[49]

At least three firms currently follow this pattern. Books appear twelve to eighteen months after the financial arrangements have been made, and the publishers issue six or seven books a year offering much the same things that D. Mason and Company, of Syracuse, offered in the 1880s. These publishing concerns organize a community's desire to have a history, which otherwise would be left to an individual or perhaps to a local institution—or might not happen at all. They make the actual book possible because of their organizational zeal and their emphasis upon collecting commitments for the book before anyone else becomes involved. They offer an attractive volume, full of pictures, with a text written by someone who knows the area and who is known locally. Businessmen support this venture as a means of advertising their companies and of promoting the community, and these books often include a special section that contains histories of local industries. Local companies are buying into a city's future as well as advertising their connection to its past.

A coauthor of such a history stated that "people are buying immortality." And then he candidly added, as a historian, "so am I." Continental Heritage estimated that 70 percent of all book sales of this type are made to the business community—many used as gifts to company personnel or to individuals with whom the company does business—and that most book sales are guaranteed prior to publication. People who buy these books are not tourists: priced at twenty-five dollars or more, the books are well beyond what most tourists are willing to spend. Rather, those who buy the books are "people who have been in town a long time."[50]

<hr/>

Local history today faces the challenge of its own popularity. With expanded visibility, and the diverse uses to which local history is put, there is a danger of commercializing our local past or trivializing it. The public seeks more from our history than entertainment. Local history today is one way of providing a mobile population, whose traditional values are unknown or lost, with a sense of place and an understanding of continuity. Will this be translated into a syrupy anti-modern belief that the old days were really the "good old days"? It is easy to distort the past, to violate its integrity. With so much "use" of local history—by schoolteachers, newspapers, chambers of commerce, in advertising, in publishing—it is possible to end up with great masses of facts but little genuine understanding of what the past is all about.

Local history has once again become the occupation and avocation of thoughtful individuals, many trained in the study of history and interested in history for what it can tell us about our communities and ourselves. Academic interest will challenge amateur historians to read widely and to seek new ways of using a variety of materials. Historical agencies will seek to represent in their archives, publications, and exhibits the diversity of the past, and an educated public will seek out the finer historical studies.

The challenge for local historians is to root knowledge of the community securely in broad research and to be open to new scholarly trends, to be aware of the tradition of local history, to be willing to retain from the past lines of approach, methods, and attitudes that are most helpful and to discard what is not. Local historians need to be intellectually honest, in order to change that which needs to be altered, and challenge that which needs to be questioned. The greatest challenge to local history is sure to come from its own popularity with people who regard it as potentially useful. The 1980s and 1990s might be the most interesting phase yet for local history writing and practice in this country, given high public interest, the opportunity for rapprochement with academic historians, and the newly available methods with which to deal with the materials at hand. The answer to this challenge surely lies in the ability and the desire of local historians everywhere to strive for excellence.

# NOTES

1. H. P. R. Finberg, "Local History," in *Approaches to History* (London: Routledge & Kegan Paul, 1962), 125

2. Anthony Richard Wagner, *English Genealogy* (Oxford: Clarendon Press, 1972), 367; H. P. R. Finberg, "Local History," 111-125; W. G. Hoskins, *Local History in England* (London: Longmans, 1959), especially Chapter Two; W. R. Powell, "Local History in Theory and Practice," in *Bulletin of the Institute of Historical Research* 31 (1958): 41-48; Pierre Goubert, "Local History," in *Daedalus* 100 (Winter 1971): 113-127. Also Rev. Thomas Dunham Whitaker, in *History and Antiquities of Craven,* 2nd ed. (London: J. Nichols and Son, 1812), v, quoted in Wagner, *English Genealogy,* 381.

3. Hermann E. Ludewig, *The Literature of American Local History* (New York: privately printed, 1846), vii.

4. *The Reconstruction of American History* (New York: Harper & Brothers, 1962), 10-11.

5. H. C. Goodwin, *Pioneer History of Courtland County and the Border Wars of New York* (New York: A. B. Burdick Publisher, 1859), 94; and Franklin B. Hough, *History of Lewis County in the State of New York From the Beginning of its Settlement to the Present Time* (Albany: Munsell & Rowland, 1860), 1.

6. Horace King, *Early History of Ithaca: A Lecture* (Ithaca, New York: Mack, Andrus, & Co. Printers, 1847), 18.

7. Appleton Prentiss Clark Griffin, *Index of the Literature of American Local History in Collections Published in 1890-95* (Boston: Carl H. Heintzemann, 1896), throughout; Ludewig, *The Literature of American Local History,* especially 111-117, for almanacs and anniversary speeches.

8. J. Cooper, *The Chronicles of Cooperstown* (Cooperstown, New York: H. & E. Phinney, 1838); J.B. Wilkerson, *Annals of Binghamton* (Binghamton, New York: The Times Association, 1840, reprinted 1872), iii-iv.

9. Louis Bisceglia, "Writers of Small Histories: Local Historians in the United States and Britain," *The Local Historian* 14 (February 1980): 4-10 (the term "small histories" originated with Dr. Samuel Johnson); John Delafield, "A General View and Agricultural Survey of the County of Seneca," in *Transactions of the New York State Agricultural Society 1850* 10 (1851): 397; and Nathaniel S. Prime, *A History of Long Island From its First Settlement to the Year 1845 with Special Reference to its Ecclesiastical Concerns* (New York and Pittsburgh: R. Carter, 1845), iii.

10. Wilkerson, *Annals of Binghamton,* v.

11. George H. Callcott, *History in the United States 1800-1860: Its Practice and Purpose* (Baltimore: Johns Hopkins Press, 1970), 87-88.

12. David D. Van Tassel, "Biography: The Creation of National Heroes, 1776-1849," in *Recording America's Past: An Interpretation of the Development of Historical Studies in America 1607-1884* (Chicago: University of Chicago Press, 1960), 66-67.

13. *Knickerbocker's History of New York* (1809; reprint, New York: G. P. Putnam's Sons, 1894), 1:23-25.

14. *Writing American History* (Bloomington: Indiana University Press, 1970), 13.

15. Wilkerson, *Annals of Binghamton,* iv.

16. Walter Muir Whitehill, *Independent Historical Societies* (Lunenburg, Vermont: The Boston Athenaeum, 1962), 350; and Van Tassel, *Recording America's Past,* Appendix, 181-190, where there is a list of historical societies and the dates of their creation.

17. D. H. H., *History of Clinton and Franklin Counties* (Philadelphia: J. W. Lewis Co., 1880), unpaged preface; and Nathan Bouton, *Festal Gatherings of the Early Settlers and Present Inhabitants of Virgil* (Dryden, New York: A. M. Ford, 1878), 2: 1.

18. Gilbert W. Hazeltine, *The Early History of the Town of Ellicott, Chatauqua County, N.Y., Compiled Largely from the Personal Recollections of the Author* (Jamestown, New York: Lewis Historical Publishing Company, 1887), v-vi. H. J. Swinney brought this particular history to my attention.

19. Higham, *Reconstruction of American History,* 10-11; Van Tassel, *Recording America's Past,* 179 and all of Chapter 19, "Denouement: The Triumph of National History, 1876-84," 171-180.

20. John Higham, "Herbert Baxter Adams and the Study of Local History," *American Historical Review* 89 (December 1984): 1225-1239.

21. *Ibid.,* 1232.

22. J. Franklin Jameson to John Jameson, January 5, 1889, quoted in *ibid.*

23. Edward Eggleston, quoted by Higham, *ibid.*; and Larry E. Tise, "State and Local History: A Future from the Past," *The Public Historian* 1 (Summer 1979): 15.

24. George W. Cowles, *Landmarks of Wayne County, New York* (Syracuse, New York: D. Mason & Co., 1895); Edgar C. Emerson, ed., *Our County and Its People: A Descriptive Work on Jefferson County, New York* (Boston: Boston History Company Publishers, 1898), iii, iv-v; and Washington Frothingham, *History of Montgomery County, Embracing Early Discoveries...* (Syracuse, New York: D. Mason & Co., 1892), 7.

25. Christfield Johnson, *Centennial History of Erie County, New York* (Buffalo: Mathews & Warren, 1876), 7.

26. Franklin B. Hough, *History of Lewis County, New York* (Syracuse, New York: D. Mason & Co., 1883); John A. Haddock, *The Growth of a Century as Illustrated in the History of Jefferson County, New York, from 1793 to 1894*

(Philadelphia: Sherman & Company, 1894); Arad Thomas, *Pioneer History of Orleans County, New York...* (Albion, New York: H. A. Bruner, Orleans Steam Press, 1871), iv, v.

27. H. P. Smith, *History of Cortland County, New York* (Syracuse, New York: D. Mason & Co., 1885), 3.

28. Harold Nestler, *Bibliography of New York State Communities, Counties, Towns, Villages* (Port Washington, New York: Ira J. Friedman, 1968), unpaged.

29. Richard M. Dorson, *American Folklore and the Historian* (Chicago: University of Chicago Press, 1971), 149.

30. (Syracuse, New York, 1892), 7.

31. Marion Talbot, "Report of the Association of Collegiate Alumnae," in May Wright Sewall, ed., *World's Congress of Representative Women* (Chicago and New York: Rand, McNally and Company, 1894), 793. See also Joan J. Brumberg and Nancy Tomes, "Women in the Professions: A Research Agenda for American Historians," *Reviews in American History* 10 (June 1982): 285-286.

32. *History of Orange County, New York* (Middletown, New York: Van Deusen & Elms, 1908), 5.

33. *Exile's Return: A Narrative of Ideas* (New York: W. W. Norton, 1934), 29,31; Callcott, *History in the United States*, 90.

34. J. Franklin Jameson to James Truslow Adams, March 1, 1918, J. Franklin Jameson Papers, Box 46, Library of Congress; and James T. Adams to Jameson, March 5, 1918, *ibid.*

35. Uri Mulford, *Pioneer Days and Later Times in Corning and Vicinity, 1789-1920* (Corning, New York: U. Mulford Publisher, 1920), unpaged preface.

36. See "Historian Man of Year," *The Ithaca Journal,* 2 January 1971, and conversations with the author; *The Ithaca Journal,* 5 January 1980. See also Helen Hooven Santmyer, *Ohio Town: a Portrait of Xenia* (Columbus: Ohio State University Press, 1962; New York: Harper & Row, 1984), 255-256.

37. *Annual Report of the American Historical Association for the Year 1914* (Washington, D.C.: The American Historical Association, 1916), 2: 304-308

38. *Ibid.,* 2: 308-314.

39. Henry Charlton Beck, *More Forgotten Towns of Southern New Jersey* (Rahway, New Jersey: Quinn & Boden Co., 1936), 6.

40. W. G. Hoskins, *Fieldwork in Local History* (London: Faber & Faber, 1967), 12.

41. John D. Haskell, Jr., "Writings on Maine History: The Story up to Now" (paper delivered at a symposium on Maine history, Orono, Maine, 5 May 1978); and R. Richard Wohl and A. Theodore Brown, "The Usable Past, A Study of Historical Traditions in Kansas City," *Huntington Library Quarterly* 23 (May 1960): 237-259.

42. See Bruce M. Stave, *The Making of Urban History: Historiography*

*Through Oral History* (Beverly Hills, California: Sage Publications, 1977), especially interviews with Blake McKelvey, 33-62, and Constance McLaughlin Green, 103-144. See also Constance McLaughlin Green, "The Value of Local History," in Caroline F. Ware, *The Cultural Approach to History* (New York: Columbia University Press, 1940), 275-290.

43. Merle Curti, quoted in Theodore C. Blegen, *Grass Roots History* (Minneapolis: University of Minnesota Press, 1947), 247.

44. Whitfield J. Bell, Jr., "The Amateur Historian," *New York History* 8 (July 1972): 265-282; and Richard Shryock, "Changing Perspectives in Local History," *New York History* 31 (July 1950): 243-260.

45. Lawrence Stone, "English and United States Local History," *Daedalus* 100 (Winter 1971): 128-132.

46. H. P. R. Finberg, "Local History," 111-125; W. R. Powell, "Local History in Theory and Practice"; Alan Rogers, "The Study of Local History—Opinion & Practice: 3. New Horizons In Local History," *The Local Historian* 12 (June 1976); 67-73; W. G. Hoskins, *Local History in England*; David Iredale, *Local History Research and Writing: A Manual for Local History Writers* (Leeds: Elmfield Press, 1974).

47. Marc Bloch, *The Ile-de-France: The Country Around Paris* (Ithaca, New York: Cornell University Press, 1971), 120, and Pierre Goubert, "Local History," 113-127.

48. Mickey Thompson, of Continental Heritage Publishing Company, telephone conversation with the author, 9 November 1982.

49. Laurence Bothwell, conversations with the author, 17 July 1982 and thereafter. Bothwell's book, *Broome County Heritage: An Illustrated History,* was published by Windsor Press, Woodland Hills, California, in 1983. On page 6 there is a list of sixty-three companies, organizations, and individuals who are thanked for their "valuable commitment to the quality of this publication." In a special section at the end of the book entitled "Partners for Progress," there are one-page sketches of these contributors.

50. Thompson, *ibid.;* Ross McGuire, conversations with the author, 17 July 1982.

# 2 ☙ Researching Local History

*This single circumstance of want of materials, would, in the absence of all other reasons, justify us in receiving with extreme distrust, the narratives of the earliest historians. Before the art of printing was invented, but few documents existed, and tradition furnishes almost the only materials for history. How much falsehood gathered in its progress, and how much truth, modifying and almost changing the aspects of the truths it transmitted, was lost on the way, could only be the subject of conjecture.*

SALMA HALE (1822)[1]

EVERYTHING THAT men and women have written, touched, or made is a clue to the past. Such a wide range of material demands of the local historian a variety of talents in order that this evidence yield up its secrets. We need to do more than simply accept the flotsam of the past: we must question it, consider it, evaluate possible reasons for its creation in the first place, and wonder why it has survived. Although this is an obvious way to approach a historical artifact, it is not one regularly used by all historians—a lack that has led to problems for even the most careful researcher. Many times, that which the past has given us controls our view of a particular era or episode. Ley me try to illustrate the problem.

Many communities (and most secretary of states' offices) have business incorporation papers for a mill, a business, or a small manufactory. The local historian, by dint of hard work, may discover a sales ledger, advertisements in a newspaper about the product, and even some of the products themselves that have survived as collectors' items: clocks, bottles, tinware, pottery jugs, and the like. Put together, this varied information leads to the study of a local business—a worthwhile undertaking and a relatively common local history project.

The incorporation papers of the company give us the date of its founding and its officers; the sales ledger reveals cost of the product and sales for a specific period; an advertisement in a newspaper may show us a picture of the product and indicate that it was marketed locally; a specimen of the article gives us an opportunity to assess it for ourselves, to feel it and describe it.

In his 1926 history of my community, Henry Abt deals with a local industry in the following fashion:

The Ithaca Glass Works, originally fostered by Ezra Cornell, was established in 1874 and reorganized in 1876. The main factory was burned in 1882 and a new one, on Third Street between Franklin Street and Railroad Avenue, was built in 1883. At the time the new plant was one of the best of its kind in the United States. There were five buildings, containing three eight-pot furnaces, an engine room, a mill for grinding the crucible material, flattening and annealing equipment, and cutting and packing departments. Railroads had sidings at the works. Nine thousand boxes of single and double thick patent white crystal sheet glass were shipped over those tracks each month.[2]

This represents the customary treatment of a local industry and is an honest reading of the extant materials. Duly footnoted, it easily passes into the canon of a town's past. There is nothing wrong with this style of history; it is typical of most of what we read. The documents have led us in this direction and we have followed them, willy nilly. Thus, by simply surviving, by surfacing from a past era, the documents mentioned above on which our business history has been based skew our attention to a particular view of the past.

But is this all that we want to know about the Ithaca Glass Works, or any other industry? I think not. I would like to know who worked for the company, where they lived, how much they were paid, what sort of compensation they received if hurt on the job, what happened to the workers when the plant burned, the ethnicity of those who worked there, the social organizations they established for themselves, and the receptiveness of management to the creation of a benevolent society or a union. At what age did workers start in the factory, and were all of the workers male? Did worker children attend public school or the local parochial school, and for how long? What were the working conditions in the factory, who were the owners, how much money did they take out of the company, and where and how did they live? When the company was absorbed by another corporation (which was common in that era of consolidation), what happened to the owners? When the company was abandoned by the parent company in Pittsburgh, what happened to all the workers? Did they find other jobs locally, or did they leave the area?

The available documents do not provide answers to these questions. If little has survived to our day about the workers in the factory, or about working conditions, hiring practices, attempts at unionization, crises resulting from pay cuts in times of depression, or even happy employees well paid for their labors and respected for their craftsmanship, that does not mean that their history is not integral to the story of what happened at the local factory. Few working people wrote letters that have ended up in local historical societies — perhaps because these letters were never written, perhaps because they were never collected. Without a letter of protest about an unfair firing, or letters of complaint about shoddy workmanship, these everyday episodes have not been written into our history. By ignoring the total story, by not probing for more than partial answers, we allow those surviving documents to shape the history we tell. This leads to an incomplete history. Workers made the product, merchants offered it for sale, and someone bought it. These are all aspects of the history of the company, but only infrequently are such varied persons or viewpoints mentioned in business documents, and therefore they are rarely part of our history.

I once met a woman who was writing the history of a small cheese factory. She knew who had founded the company and how it operated; she could explain the entire process necessary to produce various cheeses offered for sale; and she knew with some accuracy the area in which the cheese was distributed. Because the documents did not mention the people who worked in the factory, however, she never thought about them as an obvious part of her study, and she was startled when I asked about them. There were, she muttered to me, "just local women."

"Aha," says the women's historian, or the labor historian, with great eagerness. But no, insists the local historian, workers were not important because they only "came in part time and there is no record of them." The documents we use can reveal to us only what they were designed to record. It is up to the local historian to form questions that will unveil a more complete picture of the past, a past that is more complex—and often more interesting—than we will ever know if we accept at face value only that which ends up on our desk.

If we are really interested in finding out more about the glass plant or the cheese factory than what we are given, how do we go about it? After all, workers' letters are rarely found, and employers' reactions to strikes are not necessarily part of the business documents stashed in the local historical society. Where then do we look, and how do we go about the task of finding out more than the surface facts? How do we, in fact, find out what we want to know, rather than merely what the extant documents readily tell us?

In the first place, there are newspapers—and often their articles reflect more diverse information than do many other sources. For example, none of the extant documents about the glass works mentions labor unrest, but the following short notice appeared in a local newspaper:

A few days ago a number of blowers at the Ithaca Glass Works were dismissed to make room for new men. The discharged workmen made some threats and the police were called upon to protect the property. No hostile demonstration has as yet, however, been made.[3]

Another approach is to look through city directories (in which occupation is often listed) and then to seek out the manuscript census—presently available at the federal level up to 1910 except for the lost records of 1890—in order to locate workers by occupation and by place of residence. This information begins to reveal a fairly broad view of the past, of the factory, and it often offers unforeseen rewards. Workers' names, ages, and marital condition, and the value of their real estate—information that can often be found in the manuscript census sheets—added together, will present a collective portrait. Church records often corroborate this census information and may provide death dates as well. Physical evidence can also be sought: houses built for the workers often still stand; cemetery records and family gravestones are often extant; and we can sometimes come across a communal memory of a factory and its employees. A photograph might have been taken at a company picnic, or a local newspaper might list company employees who participated in a special excursion. Taking these data together, we are able to sketch a better picture of what went on in the factory and who worked there. Add to this timetables of freight trains that might have carried goods to markets, notices of bankruptcy, and legal papers. Items with dates send us scurrying back to newspaper morgues—if they exist—and the past becomes more and more complex.

Can we draw parallel pictures of employers and employees and find the interstices where the two groups met: picnics, strikes, at church, on the street? Our story then becomes richer, and gradually the past yields its secrets to us.

This is not easy research to pursue, and it does not always tell us everything we want to know, but through it we are able to attempt a better reconstruction of the past. If we follow up on the glass workers, we can look at the city directory for the years 1884-1885, which gives, in alphabetical order, names of city residents, their occupations or places of work, and their addresses.[4] Here is some of what the city directory reveals; the letter *b* before an address indicates that the individual boards there and is not a homeowner.

| Andrews, William R. | glass factory | 51 Esty Street |
| Andris, Gustave | glass factory | 70 Willow Ave. |
| Arc, Gregory | glass factory | 23 Auburn St. |
| Arc, Joseph | glass factory | 23 Auburn St. |
| Ballsizer, Valentine | glass factory | Hancock & Third |
| Barker, Charles | glass factory | 47 N. Fulton |
| Barrett, Howard | glass factory | b. 81 Cascadilla St. |
| Baur, Joseph | glass factory | 44 W. Mill |
| Bean, William | glass factory | b. 34 Hancock |

| | | |
|---|---|---|
| Bertram, Adolf | glass factory | 48 Hancock |
| Bierbrauer, George | glass factory | b. 10 Lake Ave. |
| Boland, James | glass factory | b. 6 Lewis St. |

And so on, down the list. In all there are 119 workers listed for the two glass factories in town, plus M. H. Heagany, the superintendent of one of the glass works. Divided in half, that would mean that each factory employed approximately sixty people. I do not know, however, if the companies were of exactly the same size; one might have been larger than the other and therefore might have had a slightly larger work force. Many of the workers have foreign names, but relatively few are Irish — an interesting fact, since a substantial number of Irish settled in this community during the 1840s and 1850s. One of those listed is surely a women — the secretary to the company president, most likely — and another person might be female, although the name is no firm clue.

If we chart the residences of these workers, we find them clustered in two sections of the community, both adjacent to the factories. Only one man listed had a long, and potentially difficult, walk to work. He lived two and one half miles distant on South Hill, and in bad weather he would have had an uncomfortable trip to either factory. If we then take these 120 names and group them by the streets on which they lived, we can try going to the state manuscript census for 1885 or the federal census for 1900, locate the streets, and track down even more information about them. We can determine the number of foreigners working in the glass industry; we can find out how long they have been in the community; we can learn their ages, whether they own their own homes or rent, if they are literate; and we can learn about their dependents. An interesting side note emerges from this material: while many of the community's laborers who are listed in the city directory had wives who worked as domestics around the town, not one glass worker listed a female — wife or mother or daughter — who did such work. This suggests that salaries in the glass factories were adequate to support a family. The census, by listing individuals' occupations and value of homes, can help us determine whether this general impression is true. Neither the city directory nor the census is absolutely infallible; but work in them can help us draw an interesting group picture of people so often neglected in our local history.

In at least 8 cases of our 119 glass workers, more than three members of a family are listed sharing the same occupation. This may also suggest that those individuals felt that employment at the glass factory supplied them with enough to meet their needs and that they encouraged other family members to join them. If the pay were poor, or if working conditions were intolerable, it is unlikely that a man would bring his sons and brothers into the factory.

Documentary material for any community is usually incomplete. The next diary in a sequence telling of a woman's struggle with her religious beliefs, the key letter of a series from a soldier on San Juan Hill, or a bank account book that would allow the researcher to understand a particular failure is invariably the missing link. The old woman who lived through a special event always seems to have died the week before a historical investigation of that event begins. Even if these crucial pieces of evidence were available, would we be able to understand the past fully?

Probably not. A soldier on a battlefield can only report on the action of his platoon, or of his small group of buddies near him; he does not know about the battle down the line or in the next woods. A minister can only give us his view of a church schism; even if he understands the reasons why the parishioners on the other side oppose him, he is not always the best witness to their concerns. A father can only tell us his version of his son's decision to seek his fortune elsewhere — and even if he can empathize with the son's wanderlust, or desire for larger gain, his understanding is affected by his own love and desire that his child be safe and nearby. Our evidence is skewed right from the start; we must always seek its internal bias even before we accept its testimony. Understanding that, we can go on to ask questions of the materials that we use and extend our knowledge of the past beyond the limitations of our documents. Our questions about past events, about prior institutions, traditions, and habits, should never be limited by what is apparently available. We must always feel dissatisfied with the documents we use, so that we do not simply accept what is given but seek for all that may be of interest.

There is no rule or set of rules that tells us when we have looked enough, or searched fully, or asked enough questions, to feel certain that what we say is correct. Most historians would prefer to have at least two pieces of independent evidence to be assured of any fact. Being absolutely sure about the past, knowing that you know accurately, depends upon several things. The first is thorough research, the second is general knowledge of the area and the period, and the third is contemporary knowledge or judgment about the place you are describing and about human nature. The fourth ingredient in this process of knowing is a responsive imagination about the past.

For example, in Ithaca, in 1823, citizens banded together to found an academy. That is a fact. About the academy there is a good deal of information. I know the people who were involved in the venture, who contributed to it, what the newspaper thought about it, the hopes the community held out for it, and the benefits they believed that they would reap. I have notices of the opening of classes, the cost, and the subjects to be studied. I know names and backgrounds of many of the teachers, and I have several catalogues published at the end of the school years in which the students and their grades were listed.

I know a great deal about the community and about the traditions from which these people came. There is one thing, however, that I do not know from the facts: why this small academy, in this very insignificant village in central New York, admitted both boys and girls. Single-sex academies were the norm throughout New England; even in central New York, in the larger towns and nascent cities along the major route west, academies were ordinarily segregated by gender. Yet in Ithaca and in some of the smaller communities south of the Great Western Road, we find coeducational institutions—at a time when many learned people believed that education was detrimental to the development of females. Why, in Ithaca and Homer and Cortland and Moravia, New York, were the schools coeducational?

There is nothing written in the sources that answers this question, and yet I know that I know the answer. I know it because of my work in the primary sources, because of general knowledge, and because of my understanding of what sort of place this small village was. I know it also because of what I think I know about people. In communities such as Ithaca and Homer, where there was a tiny population, there were too few people to maintain two academies. One was built, and the families who wanted to educate their children sent boys and girls to the same building. In that schoolhouse, the boys had one entrance, the girls another, and the primary classes were segregated. The upper-level courses, however, where there were but four or five students to take mathematics or Latin, were open to any student prepared to take them.

I know that this is the answer to the question of why our particular academy taught both boys and girls. But I cannot footnote such an assertion, and I certainly cannot prove it. Knowing history depends upon a great many things, and knowing with real certainty is not likely to happen all that often.

There are any number of books that discuss ways of locating and using historical evidence, from printed sources to photographs and manuscript items.[5] I do not want to repeat what their authors have already written, but it is useful here to look at certain types of historical evidence to understand their inherent internal biases and sometimes unanticipated possibilities.

### Letters

Letters are usually of a private nature and only infrequently recount great events—at least letters we local historians usually have at hand. Obviously a letter written by Abraham Lincoln in 1862 will be different from, and possibly more important than, one written by Laura Case in 1832, for she was a young woman who lived in a small rural community and was unlikely to have witnessed great events or to have met famous people. This does not mean that Laura's letter is not of interest or of value, although her letter and most of the letters we local historians regularly use are private communications among unremarkable or unknown people.

Most letters contain two types of information: that which the writer intended to convey to a specific reader (and perhaps to his or her family circle) and that which the historian can deduce. From such letters, we might discover a relationship, an attitude toward some person or event, a confirmation of a commonly held attitude or one that was contrary to the general opinion. We often discover work patterns, hints about health—of either the writer, the recipient, or a bevy of relatives—and we read tidbits of things that we do not fully understand. This more obvious or surface information is of use in various ways, depending upon the project for which the letter is to be used.

The oblique information is that which the historian may deduce, for the historian knows the larger context and the historical trends into which individual information fits. The historian can search for confirmation, perhaps, of historical trends in a private letter—trends about which the writer might be unaware while at the time participating in or observing and recording.

Laura Case's letter provides an example of both sorts of information. Laura was a teenager, writing from Illinois to members of her family who had remained behind on the family farm in upstate New York. There is chatter in the letter about family, health, friends, and the exciting trip that brought Laura and her parents to new land where they intended to settle. This is surface information, and in the case of Laura's letter it is vividly presented. The young woman was obviously excited about the expected productivity of the new land, which appeared to her as flat "as your kitchen floor back home in New York." Laura's closing is full of hope that before long the family would reunite in Illinois, where she was certain life would be easier and more bountiful than it was at the old homesite. She wrote:

This place is so new you cannot expect it to be like New York but Sister, was it as fully settled here in Pekin [Illinois] as it is in Caroline [New York] and had they orchards and privileges as they have there [the] town of Pekin would be worth the whole State of New York. Although the town of Caroline was to me, I thought, the most pleasant place I should ever see I have seen places since I left it that are superior to it.[6]

The induced information, for which the historian is most grateful to this young letter-writer, confirms early dissatisfaction among many farmers with New York land and a willingness to leave difficult, poor, or unproductive land in that state to try their luck elsewhere. Laura Case was indicative of a trend of westward migration that grew into a landslide by the mid-1840s. Her call to family members who remained behind anticipated letters written a decade later extolling the opportunities to be found on flat midwestern farmland, in the rich Wisconsin fields, or in Oregon's fertile Willamette Valley. Census figures confirm this exodus, as do local newspaper editorials bemoaning the steady decline in upstate New York population. Census figures, however, can only tell us when a trend has reached measurable proportions; that is, when enough people have left an area to show a population decline. It is more difficult, using census figures, to pinpoint when a migration began—ten years is a long time. Laura's letter helps us know just how early people were willing to leave land that they had cleared only thirty years before.

Letters of this sort tell us about the culture of the time and about the world of the writer. They document reasons for change and its effects upon individuals. They allow the historian a view of events that the participants themselves barely perceive—because they are at the forefront of that change or because they see their lives as uniquely their own and not part of a mass movement or trend.

## Diaries

Of all unpublished documents, diaries are the most eagerly anticipated; they also cause a great amount of frustration. Unlike a single letter, which is often too short to allow us to form many ideas about the writer, a diary can reveal a segment of an individual's life. However, a diary was never intended to be a historical document. Its evidence is personal, for in a diary the individual has an opportunity to complain, recant, justify, or describe events for his or her pain or pleasure. A diary is often the stage on which a wallflower becomes the belle of the ball, or where religious doubts are portrayed as moral lapses of gigantic dimensions. A diary allows an individual to magnify his or her role, to make judgments, to lose perspective, or to abandon a charade of fairness. As one diarist noted:

I had a good long talk with you, good old journal, last night, after the rest of the family were all tucked away in bed for the night, and I must say I enjoyed it very much for you never oppose me, but always let me have everything all my own way, but if you had been capable of talking I don't think you would have disagreed with me in what I said last night, would you?[7]

Some diaries lead to disappointment; others reveal to us the intricacies of another's life. There is always a sense of excitement and expectation upon opening a diary for the first time. There is the wish that the writer be observant, that he or she be a careful reporter of events and an acute commentator about people or about him- or herself. There is the fervent hope that the handwriting will be legible. So often, however, what we find inside these books are ongoing weather statistics, sometimes taken as frequently as four times a day. One such diary recorded the wind direction of every puff, leading me to suspect that the writer made weathervanes and enjoyed watching his handiwork. (Upon further research the writer turned out to be a shopkeeper; his obsession with the direction of the wind remains a mystery.)

A large collection of diaries that I received not long ago was written by a farmer whose primary concern seems to have been recording when he shoveled out the manure and slopped the pigs. Year after year, this young man mentioned little else. His marriage day passed amidst a haze of farm chores, and we would never even know that he had courted a young schoolteacher and married her had she not also kept a diary. Her entries were recorded in a book from the previous year, so she had to override each printed date with a corrected number and day. In another case, a diary writer seemed to be uncomfortable with the days that she missed writing, so she went back and filled in the blank pages. This led to a great confusion of verb tenses and some doubt on my part as to the accuracy of what was appended.

The first question to be asked of diaries is why they were written. Donald Keene, an American scholar of Japanese literature, has suggested that there are "two categories of diaries — those written exclusively for the author's own use and those written with other readers in mind." Keene noted that some diarists write in code to keep their thoughts private, while other people leave instructions about the destruction or destination of their diaries after their deaths. Rarely, however, does a writer destroy his or her own diary. "Writing a diary, like writing a poem, is often a kind of confession, and no confession can be effective unless another person hears it."[8]

Diaries also contain various types of information. Jacob Willsey was a rather ordinary man who kept a diary for thirty years of his adult life. In it he reported facts about his family and information about his neighbors, recorded deaths and funerals, recounted a murder and a theft, and told the story of his young daughter, who married a missionary and went off to India.[9] This is surface information — much of it useful and fascinating. Also included in the diary are intimations about how Willsey conducted his business affairs and notations about owing and borrowing money, lending to others, ordering goods on credit, and selling those items to his neighbors. Amidst all this, we find some interesting clues to how Willsey and his friends and neighbors conducted their affairs and how they resolved the various controversies into which they got themselves. Willsey, we find, resorted to the courts a great number of times, in ways and for reasons that are somewhat surprising. Here are some entries:

*March 24, 1835:* Had my trial with English; Knight was my principal witness; he swore he had hired English for only 1 1/2 months & he paid him for that; afterward he worked for me & I agreed to pay him & he went and worked

85 days which the jury allowed him 15$ [sic] a month, which came to 48.50, leaving a balance for which the jury gave judgment of 3.17.

*March 25, 1834:* Snowed considerable today; English came to see if I would not give him 22.50 more; I told him I should give him nothing; he might appeal if he choose; if he does not, perhaps I should.

*April 8, 1934:* Sergeant came back & threatens to prosecute for taking the horses. . . . Stevens dissatisfied about his cattle; threatens prosecuting; rain day.

*May 5, 1834:* John Hart and I cannot come to a settlement; he is as ugly as Jake.

*May 7, 1834:* Settled with John Hart on his part & Julia's.

*April 7, 1837:* Southworth has an injunction served on him to stop selling his goods & a writ to appear before the Chancellor on the 15th inst.

*April 18, 1837:* All hands gone to court at Owego.

*September 29, 1837:* McGraw taken with a warrant for Assault & battery on Woodcock; settled the matter.

*February 10, 1842:* Went to Owego as a witness in a riot suit of E. Doolittle. . . . After a trial of 2 days the jury brought in a verdict of guilty against 9 rioters. . . . The first 3 fined $15 each, making 90$ [sic] in the whole, which I hope will have a tendency to prevent such riotous conduct in the future.

*February 21, 1842:* went to Ithaca, Court witness in the suit of the New Yorkers vs. J. Southworth. The trial of John Graham for murder of Jones took all the week. Graham found guilt the 28th.

*March 2, 1842:* J. Southworth, Thos. Davies and other suit came on; staid 'til Saturday and discharged. Spend the week at Ithaca.

*March 10, 1842:* Suit decided against J. Southworth. . . . Graham sentenced to be hung on the 5th of May.

During the last third of the nineteenth century, there was great enthusiasm for keeping a diary. Strongest in the Centennial years, perhaps it came from the same impulse that caused people to write local history. For many of these writers, keeping a diary was a personal ritual, a way of marking their own lives during a period of time when the population was expanding and individuals were more susceptible to regulation than before. A student in my class at the local community college told me of his grandfather, who had kept a diary all his life. Two years before his death, however, the grandfather suffered a stroke and could do nothing for himself. He could not speak. When he was brought home from the hospital he was agitated, and members of the family went all around the room, pointing first at one object and then at another, hoping to find what it was that he wanted. Finally someone in the family touched his diary, and the old man's eyes lit up. His grandson took the book to him, his daughter put a pencil in his mouth, and the elderly man made his mark. He continued to do so, shaping a cross on a page each day until the day he died.

The uses to which a diary can be put are unlimited. Anyone coping with a diary project should take especial note of how Alan Macfarlane, a British anthropologist, has read and interpreted a diary which he published under the title *The Family Life of Ralph Josselin: A Seventeenth Century Clergyman.*[10] There are, in addition, several new books that deal with diary keeping, and they too should be consulted.[11]

Diaries and letters raise the interesting question of prying. A gentleman, the English say, nevers reads another person's mail. Most of us are delighted, however, to find and read letters and diaries from the nineteenth century in the belief that because that century is far enough away, we are not invading anyone's privacy. But what of letters from the 1920s or the 1940s, or a diary that ends last year? These more recent materials pose challenging questions for which there are no easy answers. Use of these materials is determined by the fashion in which access to them was given and the uses to which they may be put. A letter from the Roaring Twenties or letters from the Second World War are already part of history. Most of us would feel comfortable using them in a variety of ways. But what about a contemporary diary?

We have to ask questions of the material. Did the writer turn it over to be used, and if so, why? The motive of the writer is exceedingly important. I know of a woman who is keeping a diary today in the hope that someone *will* use it, and use it soon, in order to put her and her life and achievements (or antics) in some sort of limelight. Her diary is motivated by exhibitionism and is of little use to the local historian of today. In some fifty years, it will probably be a grand discovery! If the writer of a recent diary is deceased and permission to use the diary was granted, then prudent or scrupulous use is called for. In the case of such a current document, it can be used corroboratively—that is, to document a particular trend or to illustrate a point—but I would not quote directly from it, nor would I use its evidence about people or events verbatim.

## *Memoirs*

Memoirs are among the most suspect documents of all source materials. Although they often contain interesting material, they are all too often the forum for the writer creating the history that he or she would prefer. Memoirs are intentional. They are crafted after an event—sometimes many years later—to recall a particular time or place, person or situation. Memoirs are frequently found in local archives, and while some are valuable I am always wary. We see things differently in our later years than we did when we were younger, and that sometimes slants a memoir in a particular way—usually toward being cautious and protective. We all also tend to want to remember ourselves at our best. In my hometown, a radio program directed and produced by senior citizens begins with the statement that senior time is the time to throw out the bad memories and cherish the good. This may be an acceptable philosophy for individuals, but it makes for bad history.

On the other hand, memoirs can be among our most beautifully written sources; and when a good writer and observer is at work, a memoir is a fine document containing both information and attitude. I often encourage people I know to commit to paper comments about specific events they experienced, people they knew, or local places they remember.

One remarkable published memoir is Helen Hooven Santmyer's *Ohio Town: A Portrait of Xenia*—a gem of a book first published by Ohio State University Press in 1962. It deserves our attention, for it is written in a sprightly manner and is descriptive of the town in which the author grew up. Not a history, *Ohio Town* freezes in time the attitudes and habits of another era, and it becomes a valuable source for historians in addition to being enjoyable reading. Here is a small piece from a description of the area of Xenia where blacks lived:

The East End was not a slum, but like any community it had, and has, its slum districts. Notable among these was Frog Hollow, a triangle between the Columbus Pike and Market Street and the railroad. Frog Hollow was flattened once by a tornado, and its shanties went down like card houses. My sister's hired girl, two-hundred-pound Alice, lived there. The family went at once to her rescue, and found her sitting placidly on a heap of salvaged furniture in the midst of broken walls and roofs strewn about like jackstraws. Her neighbors wailed and wrung their hands, but Alice said blandly, "Ah done tol' um, mah white folks look afteh me." But at the moment of calamity she must have been badly frightened, for she had climbed out of a two-foot-square window when the wind struck, and only terror could have made that miracle possible.[12]

Still, we must wonder first and foremost why a memoir was written. Was someone encouraged by family to write an account of life long ago? And if so, what is the attitude of the writer? With caution, memoirs can be useful and rewarding, but caution indeed is needed.

For my hometown, which had its origins after the Revolutionary War, there are two memoirs of the early days. In one, Colonel and Mrs. Thayer recalled the creation of the first church, the building of a school, and formation of county government. They wrote:

At the first celebration of our national independence held in the village of Ithaca, July 4th 1809, Col. Thayer fired the first gun in honor of the day. . . . Col. Thayer was employed on the building [of the hotel] until its completion. Col. T. was the second chorister in the First Presbyterian Church in our village, and was the first chorister in the then new Methodist Church, and afterwards was chorister in the First Baptist Church in this village.[13]

This makes the village sound like one exceedingly interested in religion, and at times it was. In the other memoir, dictated to a secretary by an illiterate tailor near the end of his life, the events recalled are of another sort. Peleg Cheeseborough talked about the drunkards who fought in the streets, rowdy games in the main tavern, pranks played on strangers, and the day an unruly mob burned down the schoolhouse. He dictated:

The town was one of the hardest possible and very commonly known as Sodom. Such an idea as temperance was unknown and about the only restraint upon the morals of the place was furnished by the Moral Society.[14]

These accounts are exceedingly different, yet they are about the same community at the same period of time. Which should we believe?

The answer is, of course, both. Each portrays an aspect of the past, but each memory has been filtered through one individual's perception. The Thayers, stolid in their respectability, put all the rowdiness of that pioneer era behind them. They looked back at the steady advance of civilization and remembered those events that showed a progression from the primitive to the respectable. They probably did not even remember that drunks had dominated the streets, for the Thayers were surely snug at home, away from the fray. Asked about the wilder episodes in the town's past, they would probably see no point in "bringing all that up" again. They did not lie; they recalled the past to suit their version of what should be remembered. For the Thayers and people like them, the past is exemplary, and much of its seamier side is best left unsaid.

Peleg Cheeseborough, on the other hand, lived amidst the drinking and brawling. Even though in his more mature years Peleg was regarded as a respectable citizen—he served on the Town Board and established a flourishing business—he recalled with some glee, perhaps, and some nostalgia, his earlier and wilder days. Both accounts of the past have personal biases, but they provide a balance to each other. A few more memoirs of that era would give us an even fuller picture.

There is always need for corroboration of evidence and for ancillary material. There is also the need to read historical documents in their larger context. Documents of a personal nature add a dimension to what we know; those of a public nature complete the picture. To all these materials, and to the physical remains of products and buildings, the historian must bring a knowledge of the general area and of the contemporary scene and his or her own common sense. One writer has noted that the historian

has to use his own judgment pretty fully. When he finds contradictory stories, he has to decide which is most probable, which writer had the best reason to know the truth—or which, on the other hand, had reason to distort it; and if he cannot decide, he has to tell all the versions.[15]

## *Newspapers*

Newspapers are another important source of information, but their use requires a great deal of patient work. I once spent twelve hours reading through one year's issues of a weekly four-page paper— not rapid progress, to be sure, but rewarding nonetheless. Newspapers, especially those from the nineteenth century, are not always to be believed. Ideas about truth have changed over time, as have editorial practices, policies, and laws concerning libel. A newspaper's political affiliation was an important aspect of its identity. Lucky were those communities that harbored competing presses, for the sniping from one end of Main Street to the other and from one edition to the next at least tended to present a variety of positions, if not keep the opponents honest. One nineteenth-century newspaper in my community called its competitor a "filthy, blasphemous and prurient production."[16] The feeling was mutual.

Newspapers contain a great deal of information. Some is the news—that is, stories about local events, politics, and the vast array of personal items that informed readers about neighbors who had visited elsewhere or who were sick, specials in the downtown stores, the size of prize melons, and damage done by a recent thunderstorm. There is also a good deal of incidental information in the press: advertisements, testimonials for products, train and steamer schedules, and political mottoes under the masthead that sometimes changed with the times. State and national news were most often picked up in articles lifted from other publications or in boilerplate— packaged copy sent all over the country from a central source. There were also stories of oddities: freaks of nature, giants, wife beaters, women sold into slavery, religious miracles to be believed or not, and the antics of the rich and powerful in other places.

## *Older Histories*

In addition to these and other sources, most local historians rely upon the older histories of our communities, or of our counties, for information about our hometowns. Yet those county histories, mug books, and town and church histories present us with numerous problems. The main one, of course, does not involve organization or bias but the larger question of how their writers and compilers knew what they wrote. I do not entirely doubt most of the information to be found in the history of my county—I just cannot verify it.

Many of those early histories of our communities, especially those that appeared after the Centennial celebration of 1876, recall a past of native white achievement, of progress from primitive conditions to a state of late-nineteenth-century civilization; they portray prosperous citizens on fertile land. They are also, as Richard Dorson has noted, jumbles of all sorts of knowledge, most of it undigested.[17] These books must be used with care. We can, of course, learn a great deal from those older histories if we regard the information in them as leads—useful leads—that need to be verified in other sources. To use or parrot the material in such books without corroborative evidence leads to a number of problems, not the least of which is that the earlier historians' sources of information are often unknown.

My hometown has had three histories, prior to the publication of my history of the county in 1985. Two of these earlier histories were really collections of short articles on various aspects of the past. They were compiled in the nineteenth century and are county histories of the standard type. Both of these earlier volumes contain information of great interest to me, although there are no footnotes. These volumes focus on the development of the area, its leading citizens, and its civic advancement: that is, the creation of churches, the establishment of schools, the purification of water. The third book is a town history printed in 1926, again without footnotes although it does contain a bibliography. The thrust of this last history is business development, the origins of manufacturing establishments, production and management, good works in the community, fraternal and church organizations. Its interests mirror the values of the 1920s.[18]

In all three of these books, and in some others in my collection, I keep an "anti-index"—a listing on the inside back cover of those topics I sought within them but could not find. This is not a list of charges or sins of omission committed by those earlier authors. Rather, my anti-index works in a positive way to enhance my understanding of my own historical interests. When I review the topics that I have written down, I can see themes emerge, and I discover in the pattern of entries subjects that I had not realized concerned me, but which obviously do.

For example, on the back cover of the 1926 history of my town the following items are listed:

> Rulloff-Clark
> crime
> influx of Irish in 1830s
> American Party—Know Nothings
> Ithaca Training School
> Samantha Nivison
> cigar workers
> OAU
> Copperhead sympathy during the Civil War
> Inlet Mission
> Italians
> Greeks
> Shawanebeke-Mrs. Benchley
> Grace Miller White
> Suffrage 1917
> Immaculate Conception (Roman Catholic) Church
> League of Women Voters
> Roorback
> Tailor's Strike

This is not complete, but it gives some idea of items that have interested me and that I have looked for and have not found in this history. We can group the list by categories of interest:

•*ethnicity* would account for a number of entries, such as the

Irish and other foreign born, and the OAU—the Order of the American Union, which was a nativist organization of the 1870s and 1880s devoted to keeping Roman Catholics out of political power.

•*women's history* includes a number of entries: Nivison wanted to establish a water-cure hospital that would train women to become doctors; Shawanebeke (or Mrs. Benchley) agitated for women's suffrage and was something of a nuisance in the community; Grace Miller White was a novelist remembered for her book *Tess of the Storm Country,* made into a movie in the 1930s. The Ithaca Training School was a teacher-training institute attached to the local academy; it prepared primarily women to become public-school teachers.

•*deviance* is another category. Under it we find Rulloff, a notorious murderer, and Guy Clark, who axed his wife to death in 1832. Political deviance would account for the Copperheads, or northern Democrats, prevalent in the area during the Civil War but never mentioned by any of our local historians.

•*history of work,* something of a surprise to me, covers a number of entries. Cigar workers were mostly women and children; men sold (and smoked) stogies, women and children made and boxed them. The cigar workers staged at least one strike in Ithaca, as did the tailors.

The past does not change, but our historical interests do. My anti-index allows me to chart the historical fashions of my own time, just as I look in older histories to see what the historical style or angle was in times past. We can look in our older histories for their fashions, their historical questions, and thus we have yet another way of understanding those who have gone before us. We write the history of a community by asking questions that interest us today. We discover that our views of the past differ from the views of previous writers— people who were, after all, writing about the same place and with much of the same evidence available today. Yet our books are different; and so they should be, for 1890 is not 1990 and we have learned a great deal, and changed a great deal along the way. Simply to repeat the history of the past by reprinting it or recycling it is a great waste of human effort and resources. We deserve better than to perpetuate the biases of the past. Our attitudes today about a great many things are more tolerant, more accepting, than those to be found in the past. The history we write should reflect our own times. The future will, as it always does, find enough to complain about—we need not add to our own misadventures the outmoded attitudes and positions of another time.

## Architectural and Other Physical Evidence

Architectural and other physical evidence is another important source of information for the local historian. All over the country, houses speak of past taste, and their testimony should be considered by local historians as well as by preservationists. Street patterns, town plans, suburban development, and renovation projects have information to give: they supply clues to the culture and origins of the people who lived there before. Folklorists have interesting things to say about house styles, as do cultural geographers. Henry Glassie, in his admirable book *Pattern in the Material Folk Culture of the Eastern United States,* looked at the style of houses and barns to gain an understanding of the material culture of Americans of various places and eras. Wilbur Zelinsky, a cultural geographer, reads house styles as easily as he reads population charts and town names to define differences between adjacent areas.[19]

These techniques can be important tools for the local historian. A book that admirably reads the lessons of the land and of decisions about topography and architecture for a particular community is Walter Muir Whitehill's *Boston: A Topographical History.*[20] Whitehill detailed in words and pictures how Boston grew, what people did to the land—they tore down hills and filled in the basin—and what sorts of buildings were erected. He looked at the function of the manmade structures and the history that happened within them. Whitehill's book is eminently readable and teaches a great deal along the way. It is a book with which historians in diverse locations should be familiar.

That last sentence raises yet another concern: a book about Boston should not be out of the range of interest of historians in Phoenix and Charleston and Butte. In Boston, Whitehill's book can be read and enjoyed for its place-specific content; elsewhere in the country it can be studied for its style, its technique of doing local history, and its erudition. We learn many different lessons from a variety of books. We glean information from some; from others we find new questions to ask about our own communities; and from still others we discover successful ways of approaching the past of our own towns.

Town plans also indicate ideas about the type of community its founders envisioned and about original allocations of space for commercial, residential, and public needs. Some towns, of course, simply grew "like Topsy," while others followed particular patterns. W. G. Hoskins has written a fascinating book entitled *Fieldwork in Local History*, which describes ways of reading physical evidence of the land itself—hedges, pathways, inhabited and deserted places. While Hoskins writes about England, and while traditions there are different from those in the United States so that direct carryover is not necessarily possible, the book directs our attention to types of evidence usually neglected by local historians. How to use our varied American environment will depend, not upon Professor Hoskins's formulas, but upon indigenous solutions; still, the book is stimulating.[21]

## *Town Names*

Town names provide us with another means of understanding the past. Some names are for fun, such as Scio, New York, which comes from a railroad sign identifying a particular piece of track as section number ten: SC 10. So, too, Tenino, in the state of Washington, was derived from the number on a box car that sat in that town for some time: 1090. Other names reveal something about the aspirations of the settlers or about their earlier homes. In Groton City, New York, the tiny population expressed a futile hope that their hamlet would expand, while it also recalled their New England origins.

Altanta, Idaho, was established in the 1860s—by southern sympathizers who had the mistaken impression that General Hood had defeated General Sherman in the Battle of Atlanta!

Town names provide us with more than good stories about our past; they are clues to the cultural aspirations of those people who did the naming—or in some cases the re-naming. Fighting Corners, New York, was thought to be a name detrimental to attracting settlers, so it was changed to Friendship. Although Friendship never became as large a community as some wanted, the shift in its name gives us some information about what the population hoped would happen. My own town was once called, informally, Sodom or Sin City. Ithaca only came into general use when the community sought status as the county seat and when an eastern bank considered it as a possible site for a branch. The Sin City Branch of the Bank of Newburgh would not inspire much confidence. So, Ithaca it was.

Some town names reveal a great deal about the origins of a community, others leave us scratching our heads in wonder, and some just amuse.[22] One name with clear historical significance is a name that many people believe actually has Iroquois overtones. When New York state opened its western land to settlement by Americans shortly after the Revolutionary War, people at the southern end of Keuka Lake clashed over the name for their town. Pioneers to that area came both from New England and from New Jersey, Pennsylvania, and eastern New York. Settlers from the Middle Atlantic states wanted no part of a town name that echoed New England origins and traditions—especially those associated with public taxation for education. The two factions almost came to blows, but a compromise was struck, and they agreed upon a name that honored both traditions. They called their town "Pennsylvania-Yankee," or Penn Yan!

## Photographs

Photographs are another source of information about a locality. They can also be a cause of great frustration, for pictures often are not labeled with useful identification. We should applaud the developers of photographs who now automatically place dates upon the developed pictures, but more than a processing date is needed. We need to know the when, the where, and the who.

I find myself disturbed by displays of photographs — even historical photographs — when they appear only as pieces of art or as relics of the past. Photographic images are potentially more than art. For the local historian, they should be documents; yet only when images are set in time, linked by themes, and explained by careful paragraphs do photographs emerge as documents themselves. Photographs have much to teach us: we can observe dress, the makeup of family rooms, housing styles, fashion. We can see what people believed to be formal clothing in those posed nineteenth-century images, and we can observe people at play and rest in twentieth-century informal snapshots. We can often deduce the context of people's lives from photographs, but of course we cannot learn everything; and we must remember that for many people having a photograph taken was a serious and formal occasion, one worthy of their best dress and most serious countenance. We must also remember that it took some time to "take" a photograph, and the expressions worn by many nineteenth-century sitters were probably due to boredom or the tension of holding a pose. While I admire Michael Lesy's book *Wisconsin Death Trip,* and while I recognize the strong sense of era and theme that Lesy develops, I would be happier still if a fuller commentary accompanied the pictures.[23] "People will not bother to read the captions," some protest, and that may be true, but I believe that my responsibility as a historian — and the responsibility of every historical agency that hangs photographic displays — is to see that context is provided.

❧

There are all sorts of evidence for the local historian to use, and this survey only discusses some of the most common types. One that I have never seen mentioned is information that comes to us in the form of gossip — tidbits, little comments of a historical nature, historical gossip. Such items are often delivered in unlikely places. Once while I was standing in a check-out line in the supermarket, someone asked me if I knew that a particular house in our town was once called "The White Rat" and that traveling actors and showpeople stayed there. Another time, at a PTA meeting, an acquaintance came over and began a conversation about places in the county where a good drink could be bought during Prohibition. And once, after my doctor had briefed me about the anesthesia to be used for a minor operation, he then sat back and began to discuss the time when the police closed some rather infamous houses in our community and during one raid found the son of the chief of the police. Whatever else such things may be, they are all bits of historical gossip.

Some of the information one receives in this fashion is interesting, but not really of much use. Other things are more helpful, items known in the local oral memory but unrecorded elsewhere; such is true of the clues about prohibition and about our seamier past. What does a historian do with such information?

Many local historians simply suppress items of this sort, while others store these facts in their heads, to recall them if the topic comes up another time. But the historian then is also relying upon memory, an untrustworthy source of information; and if he or she repeats what has been said, then an item from the public memory is transmitted — this time with the cachet of "the local historian," the one person who should know!

A careful local historian needs, for instances such as these, some sort of system to help deal with oral teasers. My own scheme does not work in every case and might not suit all people, but it is an attempt to track down and make usable these pieces of historical gossip. I try to treat every piece of information as a potential clue, and I try to remove it from my memory—where it is likely to be mixed with some other piece of information or, worse still, be forgotten. Therefore, I treat oral information — as distinguished from oral history, another matter indeed — in the following manner. First, I listen to my informant. Then I ask if he or she would be willing to write me a short letter telling me the story on paper. This letter need not be long, but it places in writing what was until then simply a whisper.

Once I am at home, I also write up what I remember of the information. Then I telephone my informant to verify what I have written and to ask any questions that might fill in more details. I again ask for a written version. Then I evaluate my informant by asking how that person knows what I have been told. The information about Prohibition came from a man who had written a paper on the topic for a sociology class in 1935. The paper no longer exists, but he remembered much of what he had discovered. The woman who told me about the White Rat had lived down the street from the boarding house when she was a child and recalled watching the parade of theatrical people troop in and out—an exciting event for such a small community. The comments about raids on the houses of ill fame were made by a man whose father had been our town's district attorney. Each of these informants had a reason to know what he or she was talking about. Moreover, each item could be checked further, the necessary step if the information is to be useful.

In the case of the speakeasies and distilleries in our area, the information included the names of some people who had been involved. I contacted and interviewed them or their descendants. I also checked my own research notes on Prohibition, which included newspaper items and some interviews, to add names and locales on a small map of our city that shows where, in the 1920s and 1930s, one could buy a drink.

If the information cannot be confirmed, as is often the case, I still record it. For example, if someone tells an interesting anecdote about an ancestor who was helped when very young by someone, I write down the episode and encourage my informant to do so also. Then, as a way of corroboration, I note the informant's means of knowing—for example, that the story has passed down in the family—and then I treat it as information that is probably true and has emerged from an oral tradition.

Not long ago, in a small academic journal, there appeared the following footnote:

12. An interview with Mrs. Beatrice Goldsmith held at Cornell University, October 7, 1975. Mrs. Goldsmith works in the Department of Plant Science, Cornell University.[24]

This note causes a number of problems. The subject of the article concerned aid given by residents of my county to escaping slaves after the enactment of the Fugitive Slave Act of 1850. The author consulted a number of people, and several of his footnotes are like the one above. Goldsmith (her name has been changed) might or might not know about local treatment of escaping slaves; despite the reference to a prominent university, there is no reason given that she has any more knowledge of the subject than does anyone else. Her university connection tells us nothing: Goldsmith might be a secretary who is an amateur historian in her spare time, and her comments about the period of the 1850s might be made on the basis of what she has gleaned over the years. On the other hand, she might be a university professor of plant science who once casually heard something about fugitive slaves and has repeated it. We have been given no valid reason for believing Goldsmith's evidence—and more's the pity, because it is a difficult subject about which it would be nice to know more than rumors.

What would be a proper credential for Mrs. Goldsmith or for anyone else? We need some reason to believe the information that a person has given us. The number of acceptable reasons are many: work as a historian, family legend passed down from participants, personal observation, conversation with someone else who knew in some definitive way.

Historical gossip creates vast problems. The local historian needs these clues, but we cannot simply file them away mentally or jumble them with others. These clues need to be systematized in some fashion. Getting them written down is a start. Evaluating the source of information is also important. Finding corroborative information makes us all feel more comfortable.

Several years ago, I taught a course on the writing of local history at a Cooperstown Seminar sponsored by the New York State Historical Association. The class met daily and sessions were intense. We had a good time together. We had—I had—talked a good deal about the nature of local history, responsibilities of local historians, sources for doing local history, and appropriate topics to be undertaken.

Members of the class were from all parts of the state and of all ages. They were interesting people and all very earnest — as was their instructor. Until the last session, everything had gone along well. Then a charming man from the western part of the state asked a question. He alluded to all we had discussed during the week but then innocently inquired if those local historians who did not have vast archives and documents to use for their community's history "couldn't just make it up?"

The shock of his question registered directly on my face, and the class roared with laughter. The well-meaning man explained that his was a newly created town and that there were no archives. All he wanted to do was to see what had happened elsewhere and then create a plausible version for his home area.

The laughter was good-natured; the class had had a number of fine discussions and had enjoyed being together. The question asked — however much a kindly jab at my intensity — needed a serious answer. How do you write a history if your community lacks rich archival documentation of the past? If there is no archive at all? If municipal records are only of recent vintage?

The best answer is to work through material that might or should be available. If a town is newly created, at a previous time it may have been part of some other town or was accounted for in some way as part of a county. The records of town or county should be searched. There one might find descriptions of life in the area even though it was once called something else. In addition, there are census and other public documents that contain information pertinent to the area that is now a town. Then there are documents that have not yet found their way to the archives, material in people's attics and desks, and some of this is helpful. The most important question that such a historian asks is why the new town was created, how it came about. Here current newspapers are useful, as are legislative acts and recommendations, county planning reports, and all the papers that cover the incorporation of a new civic body.

Evidence also can and should be gathered by observation. What does an area look like, how is it divided up, where are the central points, and what role do they play for residents? Look at agricultural, topographical, and architectural evidence. Listen, too, to what people have to say about the area. Personal observation is exceedingly important to any local history, and it is often lost when we write "too close to the archive." Often an archival researcher finds written evidence and then sets out to write his or her story without keen observation of the particularities of the place. The fire brigade had to be brought in from another city, we learn in one town history. What the writer failed to mention is that the other city was eleven miles away and that the rail line did not come up to the point of the blaze. By the time the brigade arrived, the town had been destroyed.

In other words, a community with no archive, and possibly with no records, challenges us to ask new questions about the area rather than expecting to re-invoke questions of an older sort. The manuscript census, both state and national, helps establish who lived in the area in the past; the act of creation provides a focus for the present; and how the area is coping with the various needs of its citizens should occupy a historian for some time. In addition, today's historical questions borrow from various disciplines to seek answers to elemental questions about the human condition. Older questions about first families and conditions of settlement might be replaced or augmented with an investigation about occupations, transportation routes to other places, average age at marriage, number of children per family, the relationship between weather and agricultural change, the importance of markets, the way the area identifies itself, its relationship with school districts and religious and social patterns. There is no reason why local historians should not ask similar questions in order to enrich our own perception of the past — especially when traditional documentation is missing.

***

The answer to the question, "can I make it up?"— if it is a history that you want to write — is an unequivocal "no." But the question does raise a problem involving materials found in our local archives. We are often missing crucial information for understanding some event in the past. In addition, there is some question as to what historical archives will be able to collect from and about the present. Many of us, when we receive a letter, read it and then toss it out — a far cry from older times when the few letters received were likely to be kept. Even worse, fewer and fewer Americans are writing letters at all. The advertisement about a telephone call being the "next best thing to being there" fosters oral communication that does little to help future historians.

The "doing" of history in the future will change to meet these new archival conditions; but can we, today, do anything to counter these trends? Here the answer is a firm "yes," and it involves what I call "salting the archive." We must make a conscious decision on behalf of our local history to collect contemporary materials and earmark them for local archives. By materials, I mean letters received, political announcements, and other papers of a local nature that come to us through the mail, and that means a program of seeking out information from those people who have it. Thus I salt our local archive by writing to people who have participated in some event to ask if they will write about it. I encourage people to collect their letters and photographs and donate them to archives. And I seek out people who have lived for some time in the area — especially those who have been here from childhood, to ask them about growing up in our community. What do they recall about school? What about teachers? What about their leisure time? Did they hold jobs? Did they join clubs? Where they active in their religious organizations? Do they remember the "bad part of town," and why was it so labeled?

The questions to be asked are endless, and my secret — if there is a secret — is not to encourage people to write the stories of their whole lives, but to encourage them to answer specific questions and to elaborate about the topic as they wish. If our respondents think of this exercise as writing a letter to someone eager to know, we get better responses than if we give them the open-ended challenge to tell the story of their entire lives. Some people who begin with small questions work their way up to long accounts of life as they knew it at one time or another. These memoirs are essential to collect now and to keep collecting, lest we are left with xerox sheets and sale brochures as documents that best represent our own age.

⁂

Whatever evidence local historians collect and use, we must look at it with a questioning attitude, so that its secrets can work for us. We need to feel secure in what we tell others and in what we write down, for there is implied authority given when something is rendered in print. It is then hard to excise from the public memory. We need to know all that our sources are able to tell us; we must be alert to their internal pitfalls and to their biases. This is an important aspect of the job of researching local history.

## NOTES

1. "An Address, Delivered before the New-Hampshire Historical Society, at the Annual Meeting, 11th June 1828," in *Collections of the New-Hampshire Historical Society* (1832): 125.

2. Henry Abt, *Ithaca* (Ithaca, New York: Ross W. Kellogg Publisher, 1926), 117.

3. *The Ithaca* [New York] *Democrat*, 27 December 1883.

4. Henry Mente, canvasser and compiler, *Ithaca General and Business Directory for 1884-85* (Ithaca, New York: Norton and Conklin, 1885).

5. Three of the best are Thomas E. Felt, *Researching, Writing, and Publishing Local History* (Nashville: American Association for State and Local History, 1976); Fay D. Metcalf and Matthew T. Downey, *Using Local History in the Classroom* (Nashville: American Association for State and Local History, 1982); and David E. Kyvig and Myron A. Marty, *Nearby History: Exploring the Past Around You* (Nashville: American Association for State and Local History, 1982).

6. Laura Case to Mr. and Mrs. Luke Crittenden, 14 November 1832, in Carol Kammen, ed., *What They Wrote: Documents from the 19th Century from Tompkins County, N.Y.* (Ithaca, New York: Cornell University Library, 1978), 54. The original is in the Department of Manuscripts and Archives, Olin Library, Cornell University.

7. Helen C. Phelan, ed., *If Our Earthly House Dissolve: A Story of the Wetherby-Hagadorn Family of Almond, New York Told from their Diaries and Papers* (Almond, New York: Sun Publishing Company, 1973), 97.

8. Donald Keene, "Japanese Diaries," *Japan Quarterly* 32 (January-March 1985): 28.

9. *The Journal of the Honorable Jacob Willsey,* edited by Carol Willsey Bell (N. p.: privately published, 1970).

10. (Cambridge, England: Cambridge University Press, 1970; paperback edition, New York: W.W. Norton Co., 1977).

11. A particularly useful one is Thomas Mallon, *A Book of One's Own: People and Their Diaries* (New York: Ticknor & Fields, 1984). In 1985 I collaborated with a theatrical director to bring several local women's diaries from the nineteenth century to the stage in a popular presentation entitled *Between the Lines:* Carol Kammen and Carolyn Fellman, *Between the Lines* (Interlaken, New York: Heart of the Lakes Publishing, 1986).

12. Helen Hooven Santmyer, *Ohio Town: Portrait of Xenia* (Columbus: Ohio State University Press, 1962; New York: Harper & Row, 1984), 149.

13. Kammen, *What they Wrote,* 8.

14. *Ibid.,* 9.

15. David Howarth, *1066: The Year of the Conquest* (New York: Viking Press, 1978), 8.

16. *The Jeffersonian and Tompkins* [New York] *Times,* 10 February 1836.

17. Richard M. Dorson, *American Folklore and the Historian* (Chicago: University of Chicago Press, 1971), 149.

18. D. H. H., *History of Tioga, Chemung, Tompkins, and Schuyler Counties, New York* (Philadelphia: Everts & Ensign, 1879); John H. Selkreg, ed., *Landmarks of Tompkins County, New York* (Syracuse, New York: D. Mason & Company, 1894); and Abt, *Ithaca.*

19. Henry Glassie, *Pattern in the Material Folk Culture of the Eastern United States* (Philadelphia: University of Pennsylvania Press, 1968); Wilbur Zelinsky, "Classical Town Names in the United States: The Historical Geography of an American Idea," *The Geographical Review* 57 (October 1967): 464-495. For a comprehensive list of books on the landscape, town planning, and architecture, see David E. Kyvig and Myron A. Marty, *Nearby History,* 179-183.

20. 2nd ed. (Cambridge: Harvard University Press, 1968).

21. (London: Faber and Faber, 1967). For a discussion about early American urban development, see Page Smith, *A City Upon A Hill* (New York: Alfred A. Knopf, 1966).

22. George Stewart, *Names on the Land* (New York: Random House, 1945), and Wilbur Zelinsky, *The Cultural Geography of the United States* (Englewood Cliffs, New Jersey: Prentice-Hall, 1973). Both offer information on American place names, reasons for them, and the patterns in which they have developed.

23. Michael Lesy, *Wisconsin Death Trip* (New York: Pantheon, 1973).

24. Tendai Mutunhu, "Tompkins County: An Underground Railroad Transit in Central New York," *Afro-Americans in New York Life and History* 3 (July 1979): 15-34.

# 3 ✻ Writing Local History

*Identity, the truest sense of self and tribe, the deepest loyalty to place and way of life, is inescapably local, and it is my faith that all the most serious art and literature come out of that seedbed even though the writer's experience goes far beyond it.*

WALLACE STEGNER (1974)[1]

WE RESEARCH local history to learn what happened, to find out what is interesting about a particular place, to understand the past of our hometowns. Learning, however, is not reason enough: knowledge compels us to communicate that which we have learned. This communication can come in a number of ways. Local historians give talks to groups within the community and answer hundreds of questions from people near and far. We use our knowledge to illuminate the activities of preservation and genealogical societies and other organizations that have specialized historical interests. We work in historical agencies, creating exhibits and programs; we take our knowledge of the local past to schools; and we advise any number of local governmental agencies. All these activities are forms of communicating what we know.

Writing local history is another way of communicating our knowledge. While a few local historians insist that they never intend to put pen to paper, most regard the writing of local history as an important aspect of what they do—or of what they intend to do: writing can become so overwhelming a job that it is one task easily put off to a future time.

The future, however, is now, at least for some of us, and so it is important to look at the subject of writing a local history. Far too many persons who have written or intend to write a history of their hometowns have fallen into their chore without giving much thought to the subject of subjects. "What do you mean, subjects?" asks the puzzled local historian. "The subject is the history of my community." This seems like a simple and logical statement, but it implies that the historian is going to attempt to recount everything that happened in a particular place. "A complete history," a local historian will say. But everything from the past cannot be known; there are too many "everythings," and the past conspires against our knowing them all. Some documentation from the past clearly reveals events, motivations, people, acts. From other sources, we can gather implied information. We can deduce, we can extrapolate—but at no time can we know everything. We can reconstruct past events from various points of view and from differing sorts of information, but still we will not know the event itself. We will know only its reconstruction as we have put it together—with the documents on our desk and with the logic of our own minds.

A lack of firsthand information is not the only problem. Some of the documentation created at the time has not survived; thus, in a secondary way, the past has selected what we are able to know. The past has, in effect, limited our knowledge, and again we are prevented from knowing everything that happened.

The past is complex, and our evidence is limited. One part of history is usually recorded, and part has been ignored by other writers. Settlers who worked hard, fought when called to arms, worshipped on Sundays, and prospered have had their stories recorded. But they are not the only people who were present, and just because others' history has not been the one traditionally told does not mean that their past is not equally important. If we set out to write the whole history of a place, we have to look beyond our traditional histories to find out about the farmers who did not do so well, about the manufacturers who found that they were too far from markets, and about those who tried life in the area for a time and who then moved on to other places. These and many more players were on the scene, and if we want to write a complete history they, too, must be included.

In truth, it is impossible to include everyone or everything. Evidence about all variants of life in a community was not created at the time, and much of the evidence that was created has not survived the intervening years. The past selects particular documents for us to see and thus influences what we can learn. But we, too, have personal interests that serve to select documents anew. One historian is interested in local transportation, and so his or her history is full of railroad companies and steamship routes. Another historian comes along and looks at the past with a slightly different angle of vision and sees, instead of train cars and packet boats, immigration patterns, or voluntary associations, or religious organizations.

The writing of history is a continuous process of selection: certain documents emerge from the past, and that is a form of selection; historians by their own interests select some documents; and thus, almost without consciousness, the history of the local past has taken on a particular flavor.

Even if we knew everything, we could not tell everything. Were we, for example, to include fragments from every letter that has survived from any one community during the period of the Civil War, we would drown in minutiae. Instead of giving every soldier's complaints, we generalize on the basis of information in the letters about the conditions under which they fought. We talk about their fear in battle, their cold and damp tents or sleeping blankets, their foraging for food, their boredom; we talk about the ways they managed to pass the time, or how they died. To create order where there seems to be only a multitude of facts, we select those pieces that tell the story best, those that illustrate the point we want to make.

The writing of history, then, is selective, and the process of selection occurs on several levels; the writing of history is subjective, for the mind of the historian is brought to bear on the events under scrutiny. Thus we will never tell the whole story; and, sad to say, our choices are not without bias.

Our earlier local histories are compilations of facts and sometimes of chronology, but most often they are little more. The writers
and compilers of our nineteenth-century local histories listed Civil
War veterans, mayors, lawyers, doctors, and even prosperous farmers.
They enumerated organizations, they dated the beginnings of local
enterprise, and they showed a community in a state of growth. Our
earlier histories give us a great many undigested facts—useful facts,
no doubt—but without any attempt to suggest what they mean.
For example, organizations are usually enumerated in our older histories: religious societies, fraternal organizations, civic associations,
benevolent and perfectionist societies, and of course political parties. Yet the American urge to join into groups for the public bet-
terment is rarely elaborated upon. When it failed to occur, as it
sometimes did, we do not note its consequences. Older local historians
rarely made much use of the material they presented, and that which
is given is slanted to prove certain community biases.

History, however, is more than a laundry list of what happened:
history is a reflection of what we learn, in order to ask and answer
the question of what it all means. Those early histories are not suitable
models for historical writing today. Many communities and historical societies republish those old tomes, and since the nineteenth century much history has been published that incorporates wholesale
paragraphs, pages, and even chapters from those earlier books. I do
not want to destroy our older histories: we need them because of
the information they contain and for the attitudes they exude, but
they belong in libraries. When a community wants a history of itself,
a new history should be attempted.

Some say that since we have histories from the latter nineteenth
century, they can stand, and any new writing should be devoted to
the more recent period or to other topics. Some believe that once
a history is done it need never be redone, that we should never rewrite
history. This makes no sense. A history written in 1882, for example, will tell you what the compiler or writer in 1882 was looking
for—and that is not necessarily the same thing that a writer in 1992
will want to know. Women's history provides us with a perfect exam-

ple: in 1882, hardly any writer would have concerned himself with women in a community history, nor would women's lives be mentioned. Today the history of women is of interest to us all, and in writing history we look for women as well as for men.

Let me give several examples of the earlier treatment of women. In 1859, H.C. Goodwin wrote a book on *The Pioneer History of Cortland County* (New York).[2] Goodwin rarely mentioned women by name; when he did, it was usually because they survived Indian captivity or withstood acute privation. In Goodwin's book, Maria Marshall is an example of a captive taken "by a party of savages," and a Mrs. Beebe is an example of extreme bravery considered out of the ordinary for a woman. Mrs. Beebe—she is given no first name—survived alone for six weeks in a cabin lacking a door, in the woods with no neighbors, while her husband and brother went to fetch supplies.

On the other hand, Goodwin and other authors of his day omitted mention of women even where women's chores or the female domestic sphere was discussed. Goodwin wrote: "Mr. Phelps reared ten children, seven of whom are now living—three in Ohio." Mrs. Phelps's contribution to bearing and raising these children is nowhere alluded to, and I can only wonder about Mr. Phelps's actual participation in the day-to-day "rearing." Goodwin gave us another example of this same miraculous male parenting: "In 1807 Rier Van Patten, from Schenectady, located on lot 56. His children are. . . ." Mrs. Van Patten certainly carried and gave birth to these children; and she (or some other woman) most likely washed them, nursed them in sickness, and fed and clothed them. Yet it is Mr. Van Patten's move to the west, and Mr. Van Patten's land, and the children, too, are his. Mrs. Van Patten is totally omitted from the history, absorbed—as she was in life—into his history. That is probably the way Mrs. Van Patten would have expected it to be. We, looking back, see the oddity in the situation, for we, with our late-twentieth-century attitudes and expectations, have a different way of thinking about women than people had when Mrs. Van Patten was alive or when Goodwin wrote his book.[3]

These are not extreme examples but represent the typical treatment accorded to women in nineteenth-century local histories. Numerous other examples can be found. To reproduce this style of writing is inappropriate, for the nineteenth century had a particular ethic about women and women's lives. In the twentieth, we have a different understanding of women's lives, women's abilities, and women's place in history.

When contemplating writing a local history, we are faced with a number of imponderables. Evidence is always a problem: is there enough to tell the story, can we find other evidence to confirm facts, have we looked for every possible source? There is also the problem of bias, a fact of life that we should attempt to face. What is our bias?

Most local historians write supportive things about their communities. Their histories tend to be upbeat and boosterish. This is a pattern we have inherited from the past, and it fits nicely with a community's idea of the way its history should be recorded. One local historian in my state bristled when I suggested that there was more to the story than successful enterprises, upright individuals, and progressive communities. She insisted that she never wrote anything unfavorable, that she would not discuss a local bank failure, because everyone knew who was responsible and *he* still had relatives in the area.

I understand this attitude. As local historians, we usually live and work and play and vote in the communities about which we write. If we say unpopular things or make the public uncomfortable, our audience can turn its back on us; worse, our sources of information may dry up. If a local historian is perceived as being unreliable or unfair, he or she might just as well find another calling.

Local history, and national history as well, is most often seen as a success story; setbacks along the way—and they do happen—are ignored or are looked upon as an opportunity to switch from something that failed or was second rate to something that has been more popular and has endured. Take business ventures. Local newspapers all across the country in the nineteenth century announced the beginnings of business concerns. They made a community appear enterprising. When a cocoonery was opened in Ithaca in the mid-nineteenth century, the local newspaper treated this innovation with some fanfare. It recorded the number of mulberry bushes planted and silkworms imported, and then people in the community sat back awaiting silken fabrics to flow from East Hill. Instead, the silkworms shivered in the cold of a New York state winter, and what silk they managed to produce was not enough to keep the operation going. The failure of the cocoonery, however, only appeared in small print in the newspaper's columns that announced the sheriff's sales, and the cocoonery has never been mentioned again.

If there is a fire or a flood, our newspapers, and especially our histories, tend to see these disasters as opportunities to rebuild bridges or buildings. The human cost is missing if this is the story told: not every community could raise enough money to rebuild. In the same vein, when a fire strikes a small town, and the local historian writes that this gave everyone the opportunity to rebuild in brick, an essential part of the story is missing. Could everyone afford to rebuild, or were some people lost to the economy of the place because of the disaster? This looking on the bright side of things might be a good philosophy for individuals, but it is not always the best way to tell the complete story when we apply it to the past.

Just recently, I faced a similar problem. Asked to give a talk to the annual meeting of the Newfield Historical Society (is there any reason to write N— or Town X?), I began researching the history of this small rural community, not far from the place where I live. What stood out most conspicuously was the fact that from 1850 onward, Newfield lost more people than did any other town in the county. By 1910, there were fewer than half the people in the community—only 1,509—that there had been in 1850 when the population reached its maximum of 3,816. What explains this decline, and had previous historians considered the problem?

Further study and simple deduction point to several factors that explain this loss of population. Newfield's land is poor. The area is beautiful to view, but it is rolling land with changes of 400 to 600 feet in altitude. There is plenty of water, but the water itself does damage to the land and only runs along the low valleys, leaving the hilltops arid. The topsoil is not rich, and grain-farming practices of the nineteenth century were not designed to improve the soil. This is a reasonable explanation for the failure of the population to thrive, but it is not the whole story.

Newfield began as part of a special land purchase, and parcels were offered for sale after land to the north, which was more fertile, was developed. Land prices within the Newfield area were low. Cheap land need not be undesirable land, but the land in Newfield attracted those who could not afford better farms elsewhere. Thus many people drifted into Newfield only after attempting to claim or to farm better land in other parts of the county. Improvident farmers are not necessarily worse farmers than others, and those who came to Newfield seem to have worked as hard as any of the settling generation. Poor farmers, however, lack the means to put money into the land or to hire extra labor when it is needed. These Newfield farmers wore themselves (and their families) out in the process of establishing farms on their poor but beautiful land.

Poor land and impoverished farmers are still not the whole story. What came next is a bit more complicated, as historical explanations go. The failure of Newfield to develop and prosper was also due to a lack of community organization. The first settlers and those who followed them did not establish the community networks that bind a society together and give it a feeling of identity.

It is my contention that the myth of the rugged individualist is just that, a myth. He probably existed — and still exists — but most people prefer the comfort, and help, and company of others to surviving alone. Settlers did not seek self-sufficiency but rather a sufficiency of one crop or product or service in order to buy what others were better able and willing to supply. In the same vein, most people who sought new lives on new land at the beginning of the nineteenth century joined together to make life better for all. Alexis de Tocqueville observed in 1840 that Americans joined together to form political organizations and businesses, that they were "forever forming associations."

Americans combine to give fetes, found seminaries, build churches, distribute books, and send missionaries to the antipodes. Hospitals, prisons, and schools take shape in that way. Finally, if they want to proclaim a truth or propagate some feeling by the encouragement of a great example, they form an association. In every case at the head of any new undertaking . . . in the United States you are sure to find an association.[4]

What we find in Newfield, however, is at best a weak pattern of associational activity. A school committee formed in 1805-1806; most likely it came into being in response to a new state law requiring townships to establish schools in order to collect some twenty to forty dollars intended to defray their costs. Newfield's committee operated for a brief period and then disappeared.

Church associations were also slow in getting established. There were preachers of the Presbyterian and Methodist denominations who came through the community, but they did not remain long enough to gather together a congregation. From time to time a Methodist class began, but no congregation was established until the 1820s and no church building erected until the 1830s—thirty years after the era of initial settlement. The Presbyterian church dissolved halfway through the century. The Methodist congregation suffered a fourteen-year moratorium, and those other religious societies that were brought into being in the area remained weak and struggling. Churches failed individuals in their personal religious needs, but they also failed society in terms of providing moral leadership, encouraging community participation, and aiding in the development of local leaders.

In addition, other associations did not materialize. There was no library in Newfield until 1899, when several additional groups interested in general culture also appeared. No fire company appeared in the community until well into the twentieth century, despite the fact that in 1875 the center of the village burned and a fire company had to be called to come by train from a nearby city. Only when the Baptist church burned in 1917 did the people of Newfield respond by forming their own volunteer fire company.

Following on the factors of poor land, people unable to improve it or to alter their means of farming to crops more suitable to the land, and weak civic associations, the invention of the automobile encouraged some people in town to go to nearby urban centers for employment and for services that had earlier been available in New-field. The dawn of the twentieth century, then, saw an absolute decline in people and commerce in this small upstate hamlet.

This is the history of Newfield as I saw it. Was it a history that I could tell? This question really is, do we tell the truth? Do we point to reverses in the past when we know that this is not the public's perception of what local history has been and should be? Do we examine unfavorable episodes along with more positive themes when a community generally expects that its local history will be promotional and make the community feel good about itself? Do we expose prejudice, stupidity, bad judgment, errors, or criminal behavior in the past? They are certainly topics dealt with in our newspapers today, yet I have rarely seen a local history that admits these things could have happened or were commonplace. The danger is that if we do not tell the truth, if we do not admit to diversity, if we do not allow for human fallibility, we set the past up as "the good old days," unblemished by warts and peopled by superhumans who rarely seem to have faced a dilemma. On the other hand, we do not want to be run out of town!

When we tidy up the past or present it as a series of acts all leading from a primitive condition to a state of civilization, we are only telling half the story. There have been missteps along the way to the present—they happen in every community; they have certainly occurred in mine. There have been good fights lost and just causes defeated. There have been heroes and villains of both sexes in the past, and their stories should all be told.

I was once sent by friends to see a lovable old man known as a wonderful raconteur who regaled everyone with stories concerning local antics during the Prohibition era. He was known to be salty, direct, and open. He named names, my friends said, and he told the truth: a wonderful source of information for a local historian interested in that era. When I arrived at his home, instead of the genial man I was led to expect, I was met by a tense, tight-lipped fellow. Sensing his hostility, I asked if he really wanted to be interviewed. Yes, he said. He would tell me about Prohibition, and he proceeded to lecture me on the terms of the Volstead Act. What about the effect of Prohibition on people in the area, I asked? Were there really 200 speakeasies in our small city? "No," he barked, "couldn't have been." The interview went badly, and it finally ended when he sputtered at me: "Leave the dirty linen in the closet. There is no sense rehashing those things that should just as well be forgotten."

Known to his friends as a great storyteller, this old man could go on for hours telling tales. Faced with the fact that his stories might be used in the future by someone who wanted to record them, who would perhaps reveal the unpleasant—the unseemly—side of things to the public, and especially to the younger generation, he wanted to cover all that up. Leave the dirty linen alone, he insisted, and portray local events in a laundered and proper—that was his word, proper—fashion.

There is another aspect of this truth-telling: it opens the way for a number of variants to enter our history. Some of those have been touched upon, such as people who did less well, people who left a community, women, children. But our plurality is greater even than this. Most local historical societies, however, did not collect the archival flotsam and the material culture of the Irish, Italians, Hungarians, Jews, Syrians, Poles, Chinese, Japanese, and Africans who live among us—who are "us." Searching for such people today in our archival collections is difficult, and it forces us to seek other sources such as the manuscript census, church records, and other public documents. It means looking at housing patterns in a community, at architectural styles less elegant than our classical revival or Queen Anne houses (while guarding against the assumption that all such houses were occupied by native-born whites), at community patterns that are more marginal than central, and at personal needs met in a variety of ways.

The history of black New Yorkers offers an interesting example of seeking people long considered marginal by the local historian but whose history is extensive and important. In many communities, relatively little is known about black local history. The blacks' stories were not recorded, their artifacts not considered collectable, their oral traditions ignored. Even today, when ethnic programs at historical societies are put in place, blacks are often excluded.

So how do we find blacks in our local past? We turn to the census and to public records for a start. In a painstaking process, we can recover individual blacks from the past by looking at the manuscript census where persons are identified by race, by occupation, often by their ability to read and write, and by geographic location within a community. Their wives and children are also listed, and the various generations and relationships within a single household can be determined. With such information, we can move from a statement about having blacks in our town to some generalization about which blacks were in our area, their occupations, how large their families were, and where they lived. In this way, we can compile a registry of black families — a first step in beginning to know about the black experience in our towns.

The re-creation of a black past requires, in addition, a search for physical remains such as pictures, family Bibles, houses, and churches. Sometimes the material culture and the oral tradition will reinforce each other. Sometimes cemetery records will solidify a family legend. Sometimes the legend proves false.

Not long ago a woman telephoned me in order to talk about her family. Her grandfather, she said, came to our part of the state during the Civil War. Family legends about him told of his birth in Maryland to a black woman. His father was the plantation owner, who had several other children living in the slave quarters, their relationship to him acknowledged by the facts that they were spared work in the fields and that they carried his name. Charles Washington, however, was not unaware of what the rest of the slave population suffered. He was present one day when a defiant slave broke the cradle scythe he was using, and Charles heard the overseer threaten death if the worker was careless again. Family legend asserts that the slave broke the piece a second time and was shot dead on the spot.

Shaken by what they had seen, Charles and his brother, Webster, decided to flee, and that autumn they made their way north. Something of the terror of that trip could be heard as my friend intoned words she had obviously learned from her father, who had often repeated the story to her. She said that the two boys moved only at night, hiding their shadows among the cornstalks stacked in pyramids in the fields through which they passed. By day they slept fitfully amidst the piled corn, eating whatever came to hand.

Webster settled permanently in Canada, while Charles married a Mohawk woman and changed his name, becoming Charles Reed. He and his young wife made their way to central New York, where they procured a farm and raised a family of thirteen children. My friend alone remains in the area to testify to their presence.

The cemetery records verified the names of the children, several of whom died in infancy. Church records also noted that the minister had been called upon to bury several of the Reed infants. The census records, however, disputed part of my friend's tale. She claimed that Charles had come north during the Civil War—the census listed him as a resident as early as 1835. The census does echo the family tale: Charles was born in Maryland, he was illiterate, he married Mary, and they had thirteen children. After telling me about her ancestor, his granddaughter, now in her mid-eighties, pointed to a portrait on the wall and said, "There he is, you know." So legend, public documents, and a portrait solidified the existence of a man largely forgotten.

Blacks belong in our expanded version of our forebears. They are one minority to search for, but we should not confine our efforts to studies only of particular groups. To create a truly varied and accurate picture of society in the past, we have to include all experiences that help make the story complete. There is a history of the farmer or shopkeeper who failed, those who barely hung on, those whose luck changed for the worse. We are already conscious of those whose economic luck held, for our local histories are full of such tales; but there are many ways of succeeding, and that in itself can be studied. We need to know about the ill, the criminal, the insane. We need to ferret out the alternative histories and the multilayered histories that have yet to be told. No community has a singular historical past. Every community has versions of the past that reflect various subcommunities, varying opinions, various actions, many perceptions of what happened, and why.

Local history too often emphasizes commercial success, the oft-related tale of a young man who founds a business and the usefulness or beauty of his product. A multilayered history of that business, however, includes more than an examination of the source of supply or of the raw materials and sales figures. It should reflect multilayered research; it should include the history of those who worked in the factory, the conditions of their employment, their salaries, benefits, housing, and other compensation, if any. Such a multilayered history would also look at attempts at organization on the part of the workers, their strikes, their demands. These are not the usual questions asked and answered in our local histories, but they hold the possibility of our understanding a great deal more about ourselves than the simple fact that a particular town was known for the production of clocks or chairs or sewing machines.

There is one caution in all of this, however: our search for diversity is not so important that we can overlook the part played in our local past by old established families and by the traditional players on the local stage. In our rush to embrace women and Irish and blacks and Chinese, we cannot ignore the white Protestant native-born man, who was, after all, central to much of the history we are interested in telling. To eliminate his role would be to write as biased and limited a history as that which has been passed along to us up to this time. To eliminate male history or white male history would be to create an inaccurate past. So we search for minorities and the neglected, not to supplant or deny the legitimate role played by those traditionally treated in historical studies; rather, as a chord is built, we add other notes to those already in place, in order to produce a more complex sound—a richer, fuller view of the local past.

There is a great deal to consider when starting out to write a local history: selection, bias, telling the truth. In addition, we need to write clearly and to engage our readers while we enlighten them.

In all this discussion of writing local history, the product aspired to has been assumed to be a history of the community. Often, local historians simply assume that writing a local history, from the beginning to the present, is their major task. A total history is regarded as the proper culmination of a lifetime spent learning about the local past. Yet if we hope to make a contribution to knowledge—the knowledge of our townspeople about their past, and perhaps a contribution to historical knowledge in general—then a history of a town or county might not be the best project to undertake. Faced with all the possibilities of topics that might be pursued on a smaller scale than a complete "cradle to the grave" history, how do we select subjects on which to work?

Sometimes a subject emerges from the documentary material with which we work. Letters and photographs from the Depression era might spur our interest in the plight of rural people during those hard times; a settler's journal might involve us in the economics of life as we read of the lending and borrowing of money and the many uses of credit at a time when there was little specie available to residents of the area; a diary might involve us in the religious plight of the writer. Census information might dispute the long-standing view that an area had been settled or maintained by a particular ethnic or religious group. In other words, some topics grow out of existing documents and the researcher's curiosity. The local historian may be able to tell us what we do not know (as in the case of the Depression project), or the researcher may define a project that seeks to alter our understanding of the past in some way (as in the study of financing life in a settlement area), or the historian may wish to correct a long-standing but incorrect assumption (as in the census study).

In addition, a historian can begin with a problem that he or she would like to solve. One might be interested in the question of leadership in a small community: who was a leader and what made him so, did the criteria—social, economic, educational, political—change over time, and if so, how? Were the same types of people always leaders in a particular community? Was leadership ever hereditary? How would leadership be defined? When, and by whom, was local leadership challenged? These questions, and others that grow out of the problem of leadership, could form the basis of a significant local study.

When beginning such a study, the researcher needs to clearly define his or her interests, yet be flexible in both the research plan and the ultimate shape that the project might take. A project such as this one about leadership uses local documents in order to answer questions that could be asked in a variety of localities. Its importance transcends the local setting. The French historian Marc Bloch noted that "a good local history may be defined as follows: it is a question of general scope put to documents of a particular region. The question will be provided by general history."[5] What other questions of this sort might a local historian consider? There are many: the industrialization of an area, the relationship between local needs and state or national regulations or requirements, growing amounts of leisure time and the uses to which it is put, the assimilation of ethnic minorities in an area—or the ways an ethnic group preserves its own identity while at the same time functioning as part of the general population.

Another category of questions relates the locality to national events. I like to ask what effect the Civil War had upon my community and what were the varying responses people of my area had to that conflict. North of any battle zone, people participated in the era variously: some enlisted, others dodged the draft, some supported the Union but were unconcerned with the condition of the slaves, while Copperheads—Northern Democrats—resisted both concerns and wanted peace. Some women went to nurse wounded soldiers while others kept their families together at home and thought the idea of nursing strangers rather appalling. From such a study we learn that there was no singular Northern response to the Civil War, and the divisions between people did not end when the fighting did — they lasted well into the following generation.

Investigation of this nature is well worth undertaking, but all local history projects need not inform general history. Any number of topics spring from local conditions and are worth pursuing in themselves. [See the Coda to this chapter, pages 105-115.] There are caveats when embarking upon a topic. Local historians often fail to see or understand the true motivation underlying a local event. For example, did townspeople so desire educational opportunities for their children that they formed school committees, or were there state enticements that encouraged the committees' formation? It is important to understand the motivation behind an event; not every local action sprang from the desires of the local population.

Another warning should be made about undue parochialism; that is, making more of an event that it deserves. A look at a neighboring county or several counties may show that their response was similar to that in your locality. A locality might be the core of a local historian's research, but it is not the center of the universe. Local history must be kept in a broader context; no community exists in a vacuum, without at least some outside influences. The most primitive, self-sufficient hamlet looks for, and is changed by, news from the outside, and it probably anticipates a time when some aspects of self-sufficiency can be escaped.

By definition, a local historian is interested in the history of a particular area, but it is vitally important that we have a firm knowledge of our national history and of regional variations. I would not contend that local history is simply national history writ small; local histories reflect local rhythms, and the history of one place is not the saga of the American people. Local history contributes to national history, but one local history cannot stand for our collective national experience; nor do several, or even many, local histories necessarily add up to the larger picture. Rather, the history of a locality has its own rationale, which is — and this is important — touched at varying points by national events. I find it interesting to see where the greater picture impinges upon the local flow of events and equally fascinating to discover where national events have little or no influence upon a locality. To pursue local history outside the national context is to ignore reality, and such history courts parochialism. A balance must be sought between the two.

Knowing the larger picture or context helps us understand our local material. We can then determine when we are dealing with a unique event and when a local phenomenon fits into a larger historical pattern. When I first moved to the city where I now live, several people regaled me with stories of an episode in the area's past. It seemed to be the one piece of local history everyone knew; it was paraded before me with some regularity and some local pride. "Look what happened here," the older citizens said; "see what a past we have had."

The events that sparked all this interest occurred soon after the turn of the nineteenth century when the community, then in its infancy, had no public officials save a postmaster. It was a time of lawlessness, with vagrants drifting through the area, a time when it was easier to turn grain into alcohol than to ship it elsewhere to market. Drunks slept on the edges of the muddy streets, and the more boisterous among them claimed the central areas of the roads by brawling and tormenting the unwary or the helpless. What the local community remembers today about this rowdy era is that those citizens who had settled in the area and had hoped to make new lives saw this lawless element as detrimental to their future prospects. They responded by banding together to form a Moral Society in order to bring peace to their town.

Despite what my fellow townspeople believe, the assumption is incorrect that this is a unique example of eastern citizens taking the law into their own hands. In other communities in New York state and in Ohio as well, at approximately the same time and under similar situations, citizens acted in similar ways. The Moral Society in my hometown was not unique—which does not make it uninteresting. After assuming responsibility to tame and punish drunks, it soon delighted in its new-found power and quickly became lawless itself by denying to those outside its fold any semblance of due process of law. So the events remembered by the community as unique turn out to have been singular but not for the reasons generally believed. As part of a larger trend or pattern, the Moral Society gains a greater amount of historical importance. As an extreme example of that pattern, it becomes all the more interesting. Only when the Moral Society is set in its regional context does it take on meaning and can it be appreciated. I call this horizontal history: that which we seek throughout a slice of time or across similar conditions.

There is, of course, also vertical history: that is, those events or trends that are studied over time. These are patterns of human behavior that are repeated, each time not as a replica of the past but often as a variant of it. The Moral Society in its lawless form tried to control the town, with certain economic, political, and social consequences. The same phenomenon erupted in other forms at other periods in the town's history—notably in the late 1890s, when a group of one hundred citizens founded the Society for the Prevention of Crime and attempted to regulate public and private morals. Part of the Social Purity movement that swept cities, large and small, during the later years of the nineteenth century, our local Society for the Prevention of Crime aped the actions of other similar groups. The society can be evaluated as part of a horizontal pattern, and a vertical pattern as well, for between the Moral Society and the Prevention of Crime folks there were several other groups of people who attempted to regulate public morality to suit their own purposes. By looking through time in a vertical fashion, we can place the activities of these groups in a historical progression. By looking across an era, from our own community outward, we understand ways to see events in their setting and as they erupt elsewhere. The only possible way to see events in proportion is to see them in their historical context—be it a horizontal or comparative view, one that is vertical or a look at events over time, or both.

How the historian writes of the past requires care, a consciousness of the historical setting, and a degree of imagination.

What about credit? When writing local history, what about the debts we owe to authors who have written on our topic, or writers who have informed us, and those with whom we find that we disagree? Footnotes tell the reader where we have been, what we have looked at, and why we have reached particular conclusions. Footnotes give credit to those who know more than we about a particular subject, those from whom we have learned, and those who have advanced ideas that we have borrowed because those ideas help to illumunate what we are working on. Footnotes are a map showing how we came to view the past in a particular way, they tell the reader who first said something, and they lead a reader or another researcher to additional information about a subject. Without footnotes, our work cannot be checked and it will be less useful to others. With adequate or even good footnotes, we can take our place in the chain of human knowing—not at all a bad place to be.

Unhelpful footnotes are those that are incomplete, inaccurate, or misleading. They send readers to the wrong volume, refer to the wrong page, cite an author with incorrect initials, or lack critical information. Examples of these horrors abound. There is nothing mysterious, however, about a footnote. It is a pledge to readers and to later historians that what is written is backed by fact and that our evidence can be consulted by others. A scientist publishes his laboratory method and results so that other researchers can replicate his experiment and go on to new investigations. For historians, footnotes serve a similar purpose.

I once worked with an elderly man on a pamphlet-sized history. When I presented the text to him, he looked at the footnotes interspersed throughout and sputtered: "No footnotes." He believed that a historian's aim was to be read and, being a retired printer, he wanted to sell books. He feared anything that would put off the readers. "Footnotes will scare 'em away," he repeated to me at least twice weekly. The reader does not care where you got it, he believed; the reader just wants to enjoy it. "And," he bellowed, "I want him to enjoy it too."

I could never convince my friend to use footnotes, and our joint effort contains none. But I was wrong to give up the fight. Footnotes need not intimidate readers, who can easily bypass those little numbers and who usually ignore end notes included at the back of a book. The absence of footnotes, however, places a book in limbo. Unfootnoted books are not reliable as history, because we have no way of knowing how those authors gathered their information or if the books were written from "common knowledge." (Nor are such books folklore, for they lack the methodology necessary in that discipline.)

Henry Charlton Beck, the author of a number of popular and unfootnoted books about legends of New Jersey, complains in *More Forgotten Towns of Southern New Jersey* about the carping way in which his books were received by historians. Beck's books were placed, he recalled, in one library where it was the policy to loan books of nonfiction freely but to charge the reader for fiction. A critic of Beck's style and lack of method borrowed one of his earliest books from the library and returned it with utmost speed. When the man placed "the book with some ostentation before [the librarian], he also presented a fee." The librarian protested that there was no charge for nonfiction; but the indignant reader snorted, "My money says what it is," and out he stormed.[6] My elderly friend and Beck had similar attitudes about history. Both came into the field from journalism; both were interested in telling a good story, in attracting and keeping readers; and both were rather successful at just that. They gathered their information where they could and from whoever had a tale to tell. They repeated what they heard in such a way as to amuse and entertain. Neither man was concerned about the study of history or about the need for one generation of historians to be accountable to the next.

But we are. What we write about our communities will be looked at in the future by other people who want to write about America's hometowns, and the problem with unfootnoted history is that it presents a dead end to those who want to know how we know. If we offer no indication to future historians as to how or where information was gathered, and if there is no way for readers to check on a statement that interests them, our work will not stand the test of time.

What should a footnote say? We local historians are not writing academic dissertations, and our footnotes need not be greater than the whole. They should be simple and to the point. A good foot-note tells the reader who first said a thing, on what piece of evi-dence or on which several pieces of information an opinion has been based, and what gives a writer the authority to move an argument forward from one point to another. A good footnote contains specific information showing how a statement can be made and where evi-dence can be found. It should tell in what letter, located in which collection, in what archive, we can find a quotation. It should tell in whose book, with what title, published when and where, and on what page, we can discover a similar or dissimilar argument. A foot-note should allow us to unpeel a work of local history to see how the layers were built up, thereby creating the whole.

Footnotes for works of local history can be written in many styles; simplicity should be the rule for us. When quoting a letter written by Calista Hall, a historian simply states the following:

Calista Hall to Pliny Hall, 16 August 1849, in the Smelzer Collection, Depart-ment of Manuscripts and University Archives, Cornell University, Ithaca, New York.

When crediting something from a diary, the notation should read:

Belle Cowdry Diary, 6 February 1857, page 28, DeWitt Historical Society of Tomp-kins County, Ithaca, New York.

These citations show that the material quoted from, or the material that gives you a reason to assert something, can be found in these places. Readers interested in seeing the quotation in its original con-text or collateral information can write or visit these repositories and judge for themselves how the original information bolsters that which was footnoted.

The use of a footnote requires some judgment. Where there are a group of references to be footnoted in one paragraph, they may be clustered together into one note, the number appearing at the end of the block of material in the text. All other footnotes follow these basic forms:

Calista Hall, letter of 16 August 1849, quoted in Carl N. Degler, *At Odds: Women and the Family in America from the Revolution to the Present* (Oxford and New York: Oxford University Press, 1980), 211.

and

Carol Kammen, ed., "The Letters of Calista Hall," *New York History* 43 (April 1982): 209-234.

In each case, the footnote tells us where the quotation or the information can be found.

Other footnotes expand upon these basic formulas by adding the number of the volume when quoting something that has appeared in a series, or adding other useful information that will help the reader locate the source. If Calista Hall's letters were still in private hands, as is much of the material that local historians use, the footnote would state:

Calista Hall to Pliny Hall, 16 August 1849, letter in private collection of Mrs. Nellie Smelzer of Lansing, New York.

The reader is told to the best of our ability where we found the information used. If we consulted church records, we might note where in the church the records were kept:

Minutes of the Ladies Aid Society, Federated Church, Brooktondale, New York; records kept in the bottom drawer of the file in the pastor's study.

Records in private hands require us to be as specific as possible about their location at the time the materials were consulted.

There is one particular footnoting problem that most local historians face, and this concerns statements found in our town and county histories. Those books are rarely footnoted themselves, and yet they contain a great deal of material upon which local historians depend. To footnote directly to a county history, however, is to lead the reader nowhere in particular, for the writers (or compilers, as many were called) of county histories do not tell us how they knew what they wrote down. To question their source of information is not to question their veracity; but footnoting directly to one of those tomes is not good enough.

My personal rule is to use material in a county history only when I have other source material that corroborates that information. For example, in the "Four County History," formally entitled the *History of Tioga, Chemung, Tompkins, and Schuyler Counties, New York,* published in Philadelphia in 1879, there is mention of slaves having been held in Tompkins County prior to the end of slavery in New York state in 1827.[7] In an article, I would never simply cite the "Four County History" as my source of knowledge about slavery but would note that evidence of slavery can be found in census compilations, where Tompkins County is credited with having ten slaves in 1820 and none thereafter. So my footnote would include a citation to the published census figures. Such a footnote could read something like this:

"Census of the County of Tompkins," *Ithaca Republican Chronicle,* 21 February 1821, p. 3; "Village of Ithaca," *American Journal* (Ithaca, New York), 24 September 1823, p. 3; "Census of Ithaca," *The Ithaca Journal,* 5 January 1825, p. 3; and *Census for the State of New York* (Albany, 1855), ix.

It may be noted that with primary material leading the reader directly to the sources, the inclusion of the county history, where the mention of slavery is vague at best, is unnecessary.

What of a statement in an unfootnoted town or county history that cannot be verified? If it is something that I want or need to use, I would then state in the footnote where the information came from and that I have been unable to verify it elsewhere, but that even while I cannot confirm it, I have no reason to doubt it, either. Then I use the material as I would any other and don't worry about it.

What should be footnoted? There is no firm rule that covers every case. Instead there are any number of situations that require us to give credit. When someone is quoted directly, a footnote is needed. When an author is quoted indirectly or his or her material is drawn upon, credit is needed. When a fact is mentioned that is otherwise unknown or beyond common knowledge, a footnote to the source is needed. For example, it is generally known that once there were slaves within my county, and this fact need not demand a citation. When I categorically state that there were ten slaves, however, it is incumbent upon me to tell the reader why I used the number ten rather than twelve or eight. My sources directed me to state ten, and I did so with conviction. I therefore credit my sources.

A footnote is needed any time an argument is developed that coincides with an argument or disagrees with a contention of another author who has written on a particular subject.

We need a footnote when something written is a revision of previously held ideas. Any time an author advances knowledge beyond that which was previously known, a footnote is needed. When we deviate from that which has been previously stated, we should explain to our readers what evidence induces us to think otherwise.

If material used is gathered from an individual in an oral interview, that person should be noted or credited in a footnote. An interview with an old-time resident of the area about a flood or education or family history might yield useful information. An appropriate footnote will tell who told you the information used, when you were told, and something about the authority of that individual. My footnote for a 1935 flood could take one of these forms:

Conversation, 16 April 1984, with Sally Smith, who was forced from her home by the 1935 flood.

or

Interview with Paul Smith, 1935 flood survivor, 16 April 1984.

or

Casual conversation with Paul Smith regarding the 1935 flood, 16 April 1984.

This last form indicates that the information gained from Smith was not the result of a planned interview but was more informal in nature — in this case, I talked with Smith while I was standing in line at the grocery store.

Footnotes are important, and they are relatively simple to write. They document things other people have said, borrowed ideas, and items that have caused you to think differently. Footnotes should lead to sources, and they also show the transmission of an idea. They lead, sometimes, to more information on a subject. They do not need to scare a reader or a writer.

"But what," a woman asked me not long ago, "do we do when we cannot footnote our material?" She added that in some instances footnotes would be expensive to add to a text, and in other instances they would be inappropriate to add. Footnotes cost extra if they are placed at the bottom of the page, but as end notes following a chapter or at the end of a book they add little to the overall cost. "When are they inappropriate?" I asked. The woman replied: "In a church bulletin that might carry a historical announcement, in a program, perhaps, or souvenir pieces from a community. What then should be done?"

It seems to me that there are two solutions to this problem. The first is to take one copy of the text, whatever it might be, annotate it with references, and place this special copy in the nearest archive. This annotation can be done on the page itself or on an accompanying sheet of paper; or, if extra pages are sewn in the book, the footnotes can be written on the interleaved sheets.

The second solution is what I call the "sneaky" footnote. This is a way of footnoting material that usually does not receive such careful treatment. A writer of local history in the public press is a person who is faced with the problem of giving credit in a medium where editors and others would frown upon the insertion of a real footnote. In such a case, the sneaky footnote is better than nothing. This is a footnote, or as much of a footnote as possible, that is written directly into the text. It usually does little for the graceful flow of the article, but it does manage to give credit where credit is due, and it directs readers to the appropriate source.

"As Calista Hall wroted to her husband, on August 16, 1849, in a letter donated by Nellie Smelzer to the Cornell Archives" is one way to begin a statement and give credit at the same time. Another way is to introduce a fact by noting that it "appears in the section on the Town of Caroline in the 'Four County History'" and still another is to note that historian Carl Degler quotes Calista Hall in his 1980 book *At Odds*. In each case, there is enough information to get an interested reader to the right archive, where the index of holdings will lead to the letter in question, or to the author's name and book title. In each case, there is enough information to be helpful but not too much apparatus to put off an editor, who might regard footnotes as pedantic and antithetical to his or her idea of what should appear in a newspaper.

It is particularly important that local historians be conscientious about footnotes, because often the materials with which we deal are outside common repositories and therefore unknown to others. Our footnotes do more than reveal our sources; through them we share knowledge of local materials with others engaged in similar or related studies.

By writing accurate footnotes, by annotating special copies of publications that are not to be footnoted, by inserting a sneaky footnote into material not generally dealt with in this way, we local historians keep faith with those on whom we leaned—and from whom we learned—and we keep faith with those who come after, offering our footnotes as a token of openness and honesty, one generation to another. Our responsibility, I believe, is to "leave footnotes unto others as we would have footnotes left unto us." If this sounds like a hard and fast rule, so be it. Consider how much easier our task would be today if the historians who preceded us had followed that rule. I can think of no more important dictum for local historians to follow. It keeps us honest, and it is our link of trust with the future. "Leave footnotes unto others as we would have footnotes left unto us."

## NOTES

1. Wallace Stegner, "The Provincial Consciousness," *University of Toronto Quarterly* 2/3 (Summer 1974): 307.

2. H. C. Goodwin, *Pioneer History of Cortland County and the Border Wars of New York* (New York: A. B. Burdick, 1859).

3. *Ibid.*, 199, 201.

4. Alexis de Tocqueville, *Democracy in America* (1840; reprint, Garden City, New York: Doubleday & Co., 1969), 513.

5. Marc Bloch, *Ile-de-France* (Ithaca, New York: Cornell University Press, 1971), 120.

6. Henry Charlton Beck, *More Forgotten Towns of Southern New Jersey* (New Brunswick, New Jersey: Quinn & Boden, 1963), 5-6.

7. D. H. H., *History of Tioga, Chemung, Tompkins, and Schuyler Counties, New York* (Philadelphia: Everts & Ensign, 1879), 458.

# Coda to Chapter Three: Suggested Projects

HAVING SUGGESTED that there are appropriate topics to research that are smaller in scope and less time-consuming, and sometimes represent an equal or greater contribution to knowledge than a standard history of a community, let me provide some suggestions. Not all of these topics will fit every community, and some will not appeal to an individual researcher. Nor would I advise that a topic be undertaken straight from the list. I offer these as worthwhile ideas, which, when adjusted and adapted to fit a particular community and to the historian involved, will necessarily change shape to suit the circumstances. Some of these are large projects; others, smaller in scope. All can lead to a greater understanding of what contributions local history can make.

What can be done with these topics when they are completed? That, of course, depends upon how well they are done. If carefully researched and thought through, clearly written and footnoted, many of these topics could be submitted to a regional or state history journal or magazine. Some topics could be useful as the basis of a talk; others might be published as a pamphlet by a local historical agency; a few might become the basis of slide shows or exhibits.

Throughout this book, there are a number of topics used to illustrate the text. I have tried not to duplicate those in this list, and in no way are these the only topics you should consider. These broad topics contain within them clusters of smaller, but also worthwhile, undertakings. My purpose in including this list in the book is to inspire local historians to carve out topics that interest them, that can be completed in a reasonable amount of time, and that would be a contribution to a community and to our general knowledge. In my mind, it is better to start, and then complete, a worthwhile undertaking and to have a sense of having done well than to spend time re-creating the history of a community from books already published and thus simply rewriting the work of other people.

*1. What became of them?* Select an early high school class, from a public or private school in your community, and trace the lives of the graduates. Look for patterns of geographic and economic mobility, and chart the occupations adopted. Pay special attention to the women in the class. Many women taught for a period of time before marriage; what did the women who remained unmarried do? Tracing women is sometimes difficult, but often class records collected at reunions give their marital status and new names. If the school was private, as were many nineteenth-century academies and parochial schools, chart the geographic distribution of homes from which the students came. Look for the distribution of males and females in the graduating class. Pictures are often available, and so are school records and yearbooks. If the school is still standing, use it as a document to read what you can about student life during the time when the class under investigation was present. You might study a class from the same school a decade or two later, and repeat the questions to make a comparison. You may be able to take a school in another part of the community, or a school in a nearby town, and compare a class from that place with the class you investigated. Look for reasons for differences between locales, and try to explain them. In most places, a modern class is too large to study without the aid of a computer, although at reunion time you might ask to distribute survey forms that would help you deal with the greater numbers of individuals involved.

*2. Crisis!* Determine a major crisis that your community faced. This may be a natural disaster, an economic depression, loss of a major employer, or some other form of calamity. Investigate the ways in which the community responded to this time of trial. Who emerged from the community to provide leadership? Did it come from elected political officials, from religious leaders, from community leaders in general? If it was from the last, assess who these people were and how they were able to exert control. Look at the institutions that were created, or that were in place or called into action, to help ease the crisis. Assess the various paths the community might have taken at the time, and trace out the consequences of the path selected.

3. *A company study.* Select a local industry, or several industries, and make a comprehensive study. The point of this study is not to replicate older company histories but to get at information about workers, their geographic location in a community, their ethnicity, age at which they began working, types of jobs available, presence of women on the job, working conditions, unionization, attitudes of management, the items produced, and contributions to the community by the company in question. If company records do not reveal this information, workers can often be identified in city directories where occupation and residence are listed. Those areas of the community where there was a concentration of workers can be used to determine what a worker's life might have been like. See census data about work in your community, write for state information about work and workers, and see local newspaper files and church records. Do not forget that employment and unemployment are linked. When were laborers unemployed? Where did they turn for help? The papers of labor unions can be exceedingly helpful, as can information from ethnic and fraternal groups.

4. *A neighborhood study.* Look at neighborhoods in your community today and study how they grew and how they maintained their identity (if they did). If neighborhood lines changed, or if new focal points emerged, determine what they have been. Questions that might be interesting include: What gives this particular area its character? Was the area identified with a particular ethnic or religious group? What was its economic status? How has the area voted? What styles of architecture are evident, and what mix of buildings can be found? If you are interested in the oral tradition of the area, local folklore might be investigated.

*5. Political behavior.* Study the voting patterns for your city or town, or for a segment of it such as one voting district. Voting statistics can be found published, by district, in local newspapers. Look at voting patterns on both the national and the local level over a period of time. Evaluate the district in terms of economic standing and religious preferences, if possible, and see what role they might have played in voting habits. Political party records might give clues as to who was influential in the district and what the issues were. The presidential election of 1928 (when Al Smith, a Roman Catholic, of New York ran) generated a good deal of folk material, as did the fourth presidential campaign of Franklin D. Roosevelt and the 1960 campaign of John F. Kennedy. There will be local issues that also generated excitement in particular elections. Did the Ku Klux Klan ever run political candidates who acknowledged their ties to that association? Did a particular group attempt to take over a local political party? What has been the local reaction to and success of Socialist or Communist candidates? The contemporary abortion issue as it is fought on a local level is worth investigating. You might ask if, during a campaign, the national and the local issues are the same; if not, where and how do they differ?

*6. Census study.* Look at the population of your community, from the published census figures, for as long as tabulations have been made. Can you determine census patterns? If there is a decrease in population at any time, can you determine why? The manuscript federal census is available on microfilm. A project can be carved out from the material found there. Topics ripe for such investigation are literacy, number of farmers renting land or farming as tenants, family size, number of children of school age who were attending school, families with boarders or with relatives living with them, evidence of several generations of family living together, birthplaces of people in the community, number of aliens, and size of farms. Study the insane, blind, and other impaired people, as listed in the census, and then find county records (including those of early welfare agencies such as a Poorhouse or Poor Farm) to investigate society's attitude and concern for these individuals. Census work is slow, and microfilm is often hard on the eyes, but such work yields much fascinating information and lends itself to projects both large and small.

7. *Organizational study.* Look at the voluntary organizations in your community over time. Which ones were deemed most important during the earliest days; which ones continued; which sorts of clubs or organizations failed to survive? What did these organizations offer their members, and what did they offer or do for society at large? What role did volunteer fire companies play? When did women's clubs begin, and what were their purposes? How did women's organizations change over time? Were organizations segregated? Were they exclusive? Determine how one became a member and what one received for that membership. Look at the officers of several local organizations at one period of time to see if the same people were leaders in various groups. Can you find, for some defined period such as the last decade of the nineteenth century, that leadership in the community came from a small group of people? Can you determine their social status in the community? Select one organization and trace its activities and its membership over time. What role did men's clubs play around the turn of the century, and do they play the same role today? Are certain types of organizations found at one time, and do they thereafter decline, with new sorts of organizations taking their place? Look at religious, philanthropic, social, fraternal, garden, and improvement associations.

8. *Children's activities.* Can children's lives be studied over time to determine the role children have played in the family and what was expected of them by the family and by society? Look at educational opportunities in your community; evaluate who went to school and for how long. Consider other children's activities such as clubs, ethnic or religious studies, private lessons, and play. For some people, children were an economic factor in the family—how long can this be seen? Are there different patterns for urban and rural youngsters, for blacks and whites, for wealthy and not-so-well-off youngsters? Look for references in diaries and letters concerning children's activities, including work, play, and school. Can you determine, at various points in time, how society expected children to behave? Look

in public-school archives for letters from principals concerning children's behavior. Can you determine anything about patterns of discipline, both at home and at school, thought proper for children? Look at the origins in your community of children's organizations, such as Girl and Boy scouts, Camp Fire, 4-H, and Future Farmers of America. Compare local origins of these organizations with the dates of their appearance on the national scene. How did these groups get started in your area?

*9. Marriage project.* Make a study of marriage partners and patterns, using marriage announcements in the local press for a period when the population was relatively small. Of particular interest is the geographic distance within which marriage partners were sought. Does that range change for those who are the elite in a community? Look at ages of partners at marriage, using the records of local churches and county records. If information can be found in church records, private materials, or the newspaper, attempt to determine marriage customs for a particular time. This would include information about gifts the couple received, places people went for wedding trips, who accompanied them, and places of residence after marriage.

*10. Memoirs.* Collect memoirs of specific events, especially for those we are unlikely to learn about in letters or diaries. There are a number of national events, such as Prohibition, the Depression, World War II, reactions to the upheavals of the 1960s, and the Bicentennial in 1976, that could be utilized to discover the reactions of people in your community. There are also local events, such as a fire, a particularly heated election, special community issues such as building a new road, bonding a school, demolishing a local building, or protecting a particular piece of landscape, that are topics of conversation by people who remember them but who are unlikely to write them down. Letters about these events, recorded interviews of the participants, and photographs need to be collected now, before those involved are no longer around.

*11. The Depression.* This is a particularly good project to undertake, and an important one. The Depression affected people in various ways, and the community response to it was often ineffective. Finding out about the Depression of the 1930s also involves looking at how federal programs were instituted in a locality, how people responded to them, and whether they helped. This is a project that could easily be undertaken by a group of people in the community, each tackling one aspect of the era and all reporting back to the group with some frequency. Any public library will have a number of good books about the Depression to give the group some common knowledge and focus.

*12. Ethnicity.* Can you identify various ethnic groups in your community? Can you determine when, and why, those people arrived in the community and how they were received? What were the institutions they established to care for themselves, such as churches and lodges, and what expressions of their original culture can be seen? Is there a darker side to their appearance in the community? Was nativism evident? Were there anti-ethnic or anti-religious sentiments, and if so, how were they expressed? Can you determine when an ethnic group became part of the general population (not denying that its members retained their ethnicity at the same time)? Are there particular festivals or rituals observed by the group, and can they be documented?

*13. Philanthropy.* Investigate the ways that people in your community have helped the less fortunate. Such a study will look at public aid, church benevolence, women's aid societies, and human-service agencies. In addition, you will need to document the beginning of the Community Chest or United Way in order to determine why, by whom, and how it was begun. What was the local rationale for such united drives? Have they changed in character over time? What sorts of causes has a community chest supported? Are there philanthropic agencies in your community that function outside this united framework? Are there foundations in your town that serve the public need, and if so, how do they go about it? Are community tensions focused upon any particular group, such as Planned Parenthood or the YWCA? This is a fascinating topic that reveals a great deal about how we feel about those in need and how we have treated them. Can you document the shift in thinking between the time when people gave private charity and when human needs were met by some governmental bureaucracy?

*14. Uncommon lives.* In every community, there are people whose lives have been in some way unusual. Gather documentation about one or several of these people, looking for ways in which they set themselves apart and the general public reaction to them. This project could focus on individuals, or even on groups within the community, who were consciously separate or distinguished from the rest of the population.

*15. Community shifts.* At one time or another, in many communities, local patterns have changed. Can you pinpoint such a shift in your community and determine why it happened, who or what caused it, and the consequences of that shift? It might be a political shift, an economic one, or a shift in the style of a place. Many towns grow beyond town status and become cities. Often the change in political designation happens after the community itself has experienced this change. The cause might be a population explosion, the influx or the creation of a new industry, or a change in view from the parochial to the more cosmopolitan.

*16. A personal view.* For a long time, most historians have attempted to leave themselves out of the history that they were engaged in writing. Historians instead used an authorial "we" or "one," and they attempted to be invisible to the reader; they were simply the means by which the story of the past was told. This is fine. But historians train themselves, or are trained, to observe; and as a community's historian there is no reason why you cannot write a history/memoir detailing events, things, and people that you recall. As an inspiring example, I recommend reading Helen Hooven Santmyer's *Ohio Town: A Portrait of Xenia.* This is not the only model, but it is a recent one and may be easily acquired.

*17. Community chronology.* Chronologies have long been with us, and many of them are jumbles of dates and events. A good chronology, however, can be very useful. Consider compiling a chronology by topic, annotating each event and providing a reference for each entry. Yours might be a political chronology, or one devoted to community growth. This is a project that can begin on a small scale but can expand as one's interest increases, or over time, or with the addition of other people who want to help. Canvass thoroughly one sort of information—such as the records of the town or village—and then move on to other materials—such as church records or newspaper evidence. A small personal computer can make this a very easy task, as new entries can always be slipped into place and one chronology can be integrated with another.

*18. Bibliographies.* The importance of a good bibliography of a community should not be overlooked. This can be compiled to include both books and articles about the community, plus mentions of a community in tangential materials such as travelers' accounts, newspaper articles, and state documents and even in historical fiction. Prepare the bibliography by subject: the municipality, physical descriptions, architectural styles, famous people, crime, etc.

*19. Economic study.* Look at how your community made money. Consider changing land use, the decline of farmland, the loss of farms and farm labor to other enterprises. Look at businesses in your community that shipped goods elsewhere. Which have been successful? What was the reason for the loss of a local industry? What was the effect upon the town? Did your community suffer many losses during the last years of the nineteenth century, when large corporations were formed by buying up small local concerns? What did the loss of local leadership mean if a company remained in the community and yet its head office and president were elsewhere? What role did companies play in the philanthropic life of your community? During the Depression, did companies conspire to set wages in order to keep people at work or to avoid competing with each other? How have residents of your community regarded the businesses in it? Has yours been a one-company town, and what has been the effect of having one major employer? Has the labor pool for a local business come from the area, or has it been drawn from elsewhere?

*20. Study of professions.* Look at doctors, lawyers, preachers, and teachers in your community. Study each profession individually over time to determine how many people made their living at each calling, how each profession changed, approximate rate of pay at various times, who the practitioners were—male and female, black and white—and how and when they formed a professional organization. Then look at the records of the county medical society, or the lawyers' association, to see what the concerns of these groups were. How were members of these professions regarded by the community, and did that change over time? Have some professions expanded and have some remained approximately the same size, and what caused these changes? In the nineteenth century, in many rural communities, doctors often farmed. Look for evidence of dual careers. When did women enter these occupations? Look at other occupations in your community, and ask some of the same questions to see whether occupational changes are grouped at one particular time, or if they occurred randomly. Question why.

These are but a few examples of topics that are worth investigating in a community setting. If none of these appeals to you, perhaps they may stimulate you to think of a topic that would interest you and would be appropriate to your hometown. There are many other subjects to investigate. Leisure is one; others include studies of recreation, adult education, what people read, law and order, epidemics, architecture, town planning and residential patterns, changes in work patterns—especially among women—and the effect of state and federal regulations upon a locality. Was your community a recreation site, at the seashore or in the mountains, or was there some other reason why tourists came to it? The tourist industry is a good topic to study.

Some people, however, want to write a general community history, and I would not discourage such projects—these are often sparked by a local celebration or anniversary. A good study must be focused. A broad range of materials should be used, and those sources evaluated to explain why people did what they did and why events happened. A good community study should include information

about the place—its size, its changes over time; about the people—
who they were, where they came from, why they came, why they
stayed, how they lived, and when they died; their religious, ethnic,
and political identity, the organizations they formed, and the reasons for them. A community study should include information about
competition and communication: competition with other nearby
towns for people, for industry, for tourists, for dollars. And communication: how were goods shipped out, how did they get to market,
and were they competitive? How did people in your community learn
the news? What has been the relationship between your community and the state and federal governments? How have people felt
about your community? A community study should include information about the diversity of that place, and about continuity—
those things that go on and are considered community values. You
might want to ask who has run this community, and have community leaders changed, has local government been altered, and what
has been the effect upon the people here? Just what do local people
expect of their town government, now and in the past?

There are any number of questions that one might ask and
attempt to answer in a community study. It is always best to interest
yourself; then you are likely to interest others. And it is probably
best to follow through from the beginning of your town to the present
with one or several related themes. We want to write community
histories—but we want to create not souvenirs, but rather books that
will be read and that will inform our readers. My best advice to anyone who wants to write a community history is to read the histories
of other communities. Look for some written by amateur historians
and some by academics, and select from each what it is that pleases
and interests you and what does not. Reading other histories will
help you focus your own.

# 4 🐖 The Local Historian

*I summon to my aid the muse of local History—the traditions of our own home—the chronicles of our own section—the deeds of our native heroes.*

WILLIAM GILMORE SIMMS (1851)[1]

A LOCAL historian must be and do many things. If I were to advertise for a person to fill the position, my classified advertisement would mention some obvious skills. I would also seek an individual with talents only infrequently considered to be necessary for the job. A local historian must be a multifaceted individual and one with a good deal of stamina, a person who is self-motivated and happy working alone, a person who cares to get the whole story and to get it as accurately as possible.

Local historians first and foremost engage in research about their communities. They may specialize in the land transactions of early settlers, the history of transportation services in a specific place, or knowledge about its industries and products; but they generally know something about a wide variety of subjects. Even then, someone with a specific question may well find them lacking. A local historian is expected to know everything that happened in his or her community.

Local history research leads in many directions. Its aim is knowing about a place, and most of us delight in the task of finding out. We delve into old books, files, stacks of pictures—even old glass negatives—letters long unread, diaries never intended for our eyes,

117

public records, and old newspapers. The search runs in various directions, and sometimes it just runs out. Often the materials we need are not there. In success or frustration, in traditional source materials or in items we are just learning to use and appreciate, many people regard research as the reason to do this job at all. It is the way we find out what we know. It is fun, and there is a universal hope (and expectation) that out of some neighboring attic or storeroom a wonderful document will emerge. In many ways, a local historian is like a beachcomber who is happy in the search itself but delighted when an unusual whelk or star shell appears in the sand. Research is at the heart of what local historians do.

Local historians also collect and preserve local materials. Long gone are the days when we tossed out old papers, books, and ephemera wholesale, in the belief that they were in no way useful or ever likely to be. On the other hand, gone too are the days when everything was kept simply because it was local. I know of one historical society that had, for a great number of years, preserved in its collection a robin's nest from the home of a local celebrity. Enough of that.

Local historians are often asked to advise individuals, businesses, and local governments about the proper disposition of old letters and documents. Every modern-day attempt at preservation is not a success story, but we are getting better in this regard, and our municipalities are becoming concerned about their holdings. Sometimes the public comes to the local historian seeking an expert opinion about an object, building, or document. Often the local historian seeks out those in a position of ownership or authority over such artifacts of the past in order to suggest ways and reasons for preservation. We now find value in things long considered worthless and in materials a local historian has never used before. We are willing to wait and see the importance of something develop before we toss out strange or unconventional items. Local historians also attempt to educate the public: we encourage people to keep letters and artifacts to document our own times. In our use of archival materials, we show how letters and diaries of the past can be of help to those of us who attempt to unravel the history of our hometowns. The most common attitudes concerning personal documents are held by people who believe that Aunt Sarah's letters are trivial or boring and conversely that the letters they have are the potential source of a great deal of money. It is up to local historians to demonstrate the beauty and richness in an everyday diary, such as the one Aunt Sarah kept, and to indicate the importance of historical materials beyond the monetary.

The third obvious activity to note in a local historian's job description is that of communicating. This happens in many ways. It can occur merely by answering a question: "Can you tell me when that yellow house was built?" and "When did the last train come through our community?" are two questions asked of me recently. These are common queries. We are also asked to explain how to find out. Most often, people are interested in locating family information or documentation about their own houses. Sometimes people want to know how to find out about the past ownership of a piece of land or where to find information about a local product. These sorts of questions can be answered directly and are a way of communicating knowledge. [For some comments on telephone requests made of local historians, see the Coda at the end of this chapter, pages 145-148.]

There are, of course, many other ways to communicate. Local historians give talks to a variety of groups, from historical societies and community booster organizations to the Boy Scouts. Some write newspaper articles; others edit documents or write historical agency newsletters. A few write pamphlets and books. Some local historians attempt scholarly articles; others teach. Up-to-date local historians appear on public access television or on local radio shows. Many serve as consultants—for example, to owners who may be required by federal (and in some cases state) law to insure that building sites are not historically important or environmentally delicate and are properly used if they are. A good number of local historians run or are involved with historical agencies; in some states, they are the official historians of their villages, towns, and counties. Local historians plan and set up exhibits in historical agencies and elsewhere in their communities. In many obvious, and in some casual, ways, communicating what we know is the most important facet of a local historian's life. It requires a sense of responsibility to our communities and to our materials. We all know that ideas or notions are easily incorporated into the general lore of a place and are excised only with great difficulty.

❦

So far, this job description is straightforward. A local historian researches, collects, preserves, and communicates what he or she knows. Another important aspect of a local historian's life concerns reading. By this, I do not mean reading for research: that is taken for granted. Rather, a local historian must read widely for general historical knowledge, for new approaches to material, and for insights into human behavior.

History books contain many messages. There is the immediate topic under discussion, which usually draws us to the book in the first place. We read to know about the Depression of the 1930s or about the history of the election of 1860, or we read women's history. Even if these books are not specifically about our place, they enhance our general knowledge and give us the background to pursue a topic on the local level. Good history also presents us with new ways of looking at documentary materials, and it suggests new questions to ask in our own work. It illustrates the important fact that some history transcends the area or the subject about which it is written.

Local historians need to read as broadly as possible. Reading about women on the Overland Trail, for example, can suggest to us questions about times when women seized or were force to exercise power. Even if the Overland Trail did not go through your hometown, the exodus along it affected a great many people: while some decided to go west, others made the decision to remain at home. A history of the Overland Trail might not inform our particular place, but it can offer questions we might ask of the people of our area. If Pierre-Jakez Helias's *The Horse of Pride,* a book about Breton peasant life at the turn of the century, seems remote to our local history, that book can still contribute the ethnographic approach that Helias used as he integrated the emotional and actual lives of the people about whom he wrote. His union of materials helps us formulate new questions and aids us in seeing the uses of slightly unusual, and somewhat difficult, information.[2]

By reading other authors, we learn how they have organized their materials, what questions they believed to be important, how they structured narratives, where and how they differed in emphasis or tone from those who wrote about the area or the topic before them. And we become better historians.

If I were to look only at the histories of my town or county for models of how to do local history, I would produce sad history indeed. Instead of disdaining a book because it is about another place, we should use it to help our own work grow. I might not read every word of a book about a place other than my own, but I certainly look at a wide range of local and academic histories in order to judge how best to tell the story of the place where I live.

Reading also helps us to understand state and regional variations, which then can be tested in a local setting: while regions may have common attitudes and a shared history, within a region a great deal of variation can be found. Consequently, I would add reading to a list of the primary activities that go into a local historian's job description.

What else should we stress in writing that job description? There are some additional attributes a local historian should exhibit: curiosity, a degree of involvement with contemporary life, and imagination. We want a person who is curious about the past, interested in seeking out when and who and also why and how and with what result or effect. We want to search out past attitudes and the texture of other times along with chronology. We seek to know what happened over time. We are interested in the human condition in our special towns and villages, in time and throughout time—from the era of settlement to today.

We hope that a local historian is involved and knows his or her community as a participant and as an observer, for that is the best way to see and understand the dynamics of a place. Understanding how things work (or do not work) today can help us to see beyond the smooth appearances of an event to try to re-create its complexity. In my community, streets were paved in the center part of the city in 1894, and that appears to be enough of a statement to cover the event. Yet beneath the surface of that statement is the problem of what to do beneath the surface of the pavement—for inadequate provision was made for the installation of sewers, which were badly needed. Knowing the problems my community has in making up its mind today about what it wants to do with a proposed improved highway, I am mindful and more conscious of the confusions that attended the approval of paving our streets. Marc Bloch wrote that he frankly mistrusted the historian "who has no inclination to observe the men, the things, or the events around him," for such a person will become only a "useful antiquarian."[3] Our local historian wants to be more than that, and contemporary knowledge informs our understanding of the past.

So, too, does the imagination. Theodore Zeldin has written that "imagination is. . . as important to historians as new documents."[4] I would not go quite so far, but a document is worthless to us without the use of our imagination. A local historian can do research and sit down to write a history or an article, but if he or she does not apply imagination to the material at hand, the result is faint. Without the use of our imagination, paired with contemporary knowledge, we fail to ask ancillary questions or to seek other causes that would illuminate what we want to know. Using imagination does not mean "making it up." It does mean that we can extrapolate from the given information something about the texture of life, something about the dilemmas faced by real individuals, something about the interweavings of events and emotions and styles to create—or re-create—a richer approximation of the story to be told. If the letter on our desk is one from a soldier in World War I who has faced gas attacks on the Marne, he need not write explicitly of his fear and confusion: we can imagine it. We can also imagine the frightened response to this letter his mother or sweetheart had. A local historian without imagination is not an unthinkable idea. There have been plenty of them. A local historian who uses a controlled imaginative approach to history brings to the story a special, individual sensibility.

Another characteristic we should look for in our local historian is open-mindedness and a sense of fairness. We cannot suppress material because we do not like it. We cannot ignore material because it does not fit set ideas, ours or anyone else's. We cannot be blind to contradictions that emerge. Often the written documents fail to substantiate an oral tradition; such a discrepancy cannot be overlooked. Instead, such inconsistencies need investigation and the "wrong" or long accepted, but untrue, version should be challenged or explained.

Our local historian should see particularity and specificity in the past, but these should be placed in an appropriate context. Thus a local historian turns a microscope on a geographic area to see how events known elsewhere were played out on this smaller stage. The good local historian is one who balances the delight of knowing particular things about a locality with a broad knowledge of regional and national history, so that events of one's town are placed in perspective. Not every local event is unique — but some are. It takes a knowledgeable historian to distinguish between the two and to know when to see a general pattern and when to claim something truly unusual. This balance is a very important aspect of what the local historian must do. It is a task that calls for both microscope, to see particular events, and telescope, to see general patterns. A. F. C. Wallace, in his study of Rockdale, Pennsylvania, looked for what was distinctive about that community and what was part of a shared experience.[5] His book transcends the locality about which he wrote, and it is a book from which we can all learn. Wallace looked at a mill town to discover what mechanized industry meant to workers and mill owners. In his book, he discusses emigration patterns, what the acquisition of capital meant and how it was acquired, and how the Christian ethic was perpetuated in the years before the Civil War.

My want ad for a local historian would, therefore, look something like this:

WANTED: Local Historian, skilled at reading history, asking questions, using historical imagination; needs knowledge of how to collect and preserve historical materials and how to pursue historical research; strong communication skills. Knowledge of community important; open-mindedness, fairness, and perseverance necessary.

Just what are the working conditions our newly hired (or self-generated) local historian might expect; under what conditions do we labor? There is no easy answer to this question, for local historians, as distinct from historical agency employees, are of many different sorts. In some states, there is a system of appointed municipal historians, paid from nothing to a full-time salary. In other places, historians are self-appointed and do the job as an avocation because they love it. They are truly amateurs, in the very best sense. In most cases, they derive very little money from doing local history, and generally they do not expect remuneration. There are also a few individuals who maintain themselves by lecturing, teaching, and writing about local history. And there are many local historians who work for and manage historical agencies.

What other conditions obtain? Many individuals do not generate projects of their own but respond to those that come their way. These are people to whom their communities look for talks, and ideas, and advice. Many of these individuals find that it is enough to preserve and organize the manuscript material that is at hand — either papers given to them by community members or documents held in local archives — and to answer the genealogical questions that seem always to appear. Some vary this pattern by collecting material about their municipalities from local newspapers, keeping a scrapbook record of current events. Others attempt indexing programs to pull from old newspapers or an old unindexed history book the names of all who are mentioned. Some local historians have told me that they spend anywhere from two to twenty hours a week minding the history of their hometowns. For unpaid volunteers, which many of them are, this is a significant contribution. Other local historians spend considerably more time. Some of it is devoted to the activities of a local historical society; in other cases, historians pursue particular projects on their own. Some work for local governments, some for school systems where they teach local history to grade-school or junior-high-age children.

Most of the work done on behalf of local history is done alone. There are only a few—and certainly not enough—local historians joined into regular groups whose purpose is to further their common aims and knowledge.

One consequence of this singularity is that few local historians look to their peers in other locales for shared knowledge, critical readings of materials ready for the press, and discussions of common woes and pleasures. This solitary way of functioning has several drawbacks. Without regularly meeting with peers, a local historian sees his or her material as a pool of knowledge that bubbled up from a single spring, rather than thinking of events in one community as having ever expanding rings, as when a stone is tossed into a calm pond. A local historian functioning within the "bubble up" model tends to research the history of his or her community, write it, and publish it, without the benefit of discussions with others and without the benefit of comparing events and times between communities.

Those people who function within a regional network of historians have, I think, a better situation. Meeting frequently and discussing work in progress, one can gain from others variations of events under study. If, for example, a group of historians discusses a particular historical trend, each individual can contribute examples. Such knowledge arms the local historian to make better generalizations and results in a comparative study of somewhat greater worth. Such a group can also undertake projects in concert, each member contributing a local example to the general discussion. In this way, each individual speaks from the strength of his or her research, and all benefit. A great number of interesting and important topics can be tested in this fashion, each historian gaining a greater perspective than he or she would have working alone.

What are some examples of projects that a group of regional historians might consider? Working in concert, such a group might look for:

•regional settlement patterns for individual communities

•reaction to political events, such as a presidential election or the passage of the Eighteenth Amendment to the Constitution (which brought about Prohibition)

•local reaction to the passage of the Nineteenth Amendment (which gave women the right to vote)

•patterns of ethnicity, and local citizens' reaction to the appearance of people unlike themselves

•examples of attitudes about philanthropy, care for the indigent, or alcoholics

•local attitudes concerning birth control

•community reaction to a shared disaster—a flood or hurricane, perhaps

•folklore investigations concerning weather, local expressions, regional celebrations, or festivals

•examples of local culture: Chautauqua lecture series; attitudes about theatre; the appearance of local baseball clubs; the formation of private and public libraries; local dramatic companies; opera associations or orchestras.

Work in progress—that is, a manuscript destined for the printer—is most often the product of a historian working alone. Few pieces of local history, published by an author or by a historical society, are read in manuscript and critiqued by others. One problem is that the word "critical" as in "critical reading" is off-putting. Yet a critical reading need not be negative in character; it can have a very positive effect upon a manuscript. A local historian from a nearby area has a great deal of perspective on the general questions raised in a community history, even if he or she does not know the particularities of the place in question. Style, too, can always be improved and is apt to benefit if a manuscript is read by someone other than the author—or the author's mother.

Another bonus in sharing knowledge and problems with a group of nearby historians is that they, more than anyone else, know the frustrations and can savor the triumphs of being a local historian. A newly found document that helps to solve a thorny problem rarely elicits more than a "that's nice, dear," from friends and relatives; but among your peers, your joy at solving one piece of the puzzle of the past is shared by those who understand.

I surveyed a group of historians I had taught one summer in Cooperstown, New York. "What do you need?" I asked. Their answers were revealing. Some wanted discussions of the sort we had had all week, on a regular basis, with other local historians. Others wanted a newsletter directed at their needs, discussing ways of doing local history, problems encountered by local historians, recommendations of books to read and the reasons why those books could help them, and explanations of what academic historians are doing that should be of interest and concern to them.

One man wanted some definite goals he should be attempting to meet. He wanted help defining priorities. What was most important? he asked. Should he locate all possible manuscript materials or engage in writing the community's history? Was a community bibliography an important undertaking, or should he spend his time documenting a local landmark? While one might want to encourage this man to do all these things, time is limited, and our efforts are easily scattered. I thought the man in question wise in looking for priorities. My suggestion to him was that he select the project he thought he could accomplish the best—and that which interested him the most. Then he might enlist others from his township to help with some of the other tasks, so that several of these important projects could go forward.

Another member of the class thought that some prizes or awards, or recognition, might be offered for local history that is well done. Some local and state historical associations offer such awards. For example, the San Diego Historical Society offers a number of prizes at its annual Institute of History, in a variety of fields of local history, and amateur historians are often recipients. The American Association for State and Local History has also had an awards program to acknowledge outstanding work by those who labor on behalf of local history; and regional associations of history, such as the Regional Council of Historical Agencies in central New York, grant awards for work well done. Yet these examples are but a few instances, and awards programs are important means for spurring on everyone's efforts. These answers to my question touch upon some of the other consequences of the fact that local historians tend to research alone, bring manuscripts to completion, and then often publish themselves.

෯

There are also occupational hazards in being a local historian, and they should be considered. The first hazard is that local historians research and write the history of the communities in which they live. Most academic, or professional, historians do not remain long in, or write extensively or exclusively about, one community. If they do write a community history at one time, their next work is apt to be on another subject. Rarely will an academic or professional historian pursue the history of one community throughout an entire career, although the exception that proves the rule might be Blake McKelvey, who lived in Rochester, New York, for many years and wrote extensively about that city. Academic historians have a broader range from which to draw documentary resources, and they often do not live amidst the people about whom they write. The local historian's closeness to his or her subject has its dividends and its drawbacks. Among the benefits are these: rarely do local historians have to travel far for their sources of information, for most are close to home. The local historian knows the terrain and understands the close meaning of words and expressions that people in the area use, which might take an outsider a while to master. The local historian knows the probable places to look for evidence and often has fairly easy access to documents held in private hands. The local historian tends to be known and trusted by people in the area and is known to them. (In a factionalized community, the local historian, like everyone else, must cope the best he or she can.)

This familiarity, however, is sometimes disadvantageous, for people in a locality expect that their history will be written in certain standard (and promotional) ways. Few local historians care to broach topics about which there is community silence, for were they to do so, the consequences could be extreme. The loss of local trust might put a historian out of business, because sources and support and new materials can easily be withheld from someone believed to have violated a town's sense of propriety. The community, in effect, expects local history to be boosterish, and often local historians not only accept this view but allow it to color the type and range of topics on which they work.

Of course, this is not to say that local historians are interested in gossip, or dirty linen. As one local historian wrote to me not long ago, most people in a community know whatever dirty linen there is, long before the local historian goes to work. We might be historical detectives, but we are not interested in hurting people or in gossip. Where is the line that we must observe between historical fact and personal information? What subjects can and should a local historian pursue?

To illustrate the problem, let me describe a recent situation. A friend brought me a set of papers that turned out to be reports, letters, and newsletters from the 1920s and 1930s concerning a local chapter of the Ku Klux Klan. The reports were of local Klan meetings, and they discussed membership, collection of dues, and election of officers. Very little was ever decided at these meetings. One decision was to support a local Klan picnic with a small subsidy; another had to do with combining with a nearby chapter — neither had very many members; and a third was a vote to have coffee and hot dogs at the next meeting — and to invite the ladies.

The Klan in the North was, from 1927 through 1933, on the decline. To many people, the ideas and tactics espoused by Klan members were repugnant, and a series of newspaper exposes had charged the Klan with murder and torture. It is interesting, then, to find a Klan still in operation, still hoping to recruit more members keeping Klan ideals alive. These Klan papers are an interesting and important find.

What does the local historian do with the information such papers contain? Many people believe that discussion of a group that is so out of favor today is distasteful. Others think such topics should best be avoided: dirty linen—that which is best left alone. But the fact that we had, in our county, such a group—in fact one of several chapters—must be faced. Some people believed in the principles of the Klan, and some were interested enough to join their activities, don white robes, and burn crosses. This too is part of our past. Since it makes people—those who participated and those who want to remember the past as "nice"—uncomfortable, should local historians ignore such items of history? I think not. However, deciding to investigate the Klan, and perhaps to write about it, is only the first step. Just how much of the story do we tell? Do we censor the materials in order to protect reputations, and perhaps relatives? My decision was to go ahead with the story, to tell what the Klan chapter did, how many members there were, the names of the offices, the oaths sworn when new members were accepted, and the fact that some members were suspended for non-payment of dues. I took the membership roster and made a profile of Klan members: their occupations, areas of residence, ages, relationship to other Klan members. But I refrained from naming names—those people I had identified were relegated to my file notes on the Klan, and their identity will be there for future researchers should anyone want to look another time at the subject.

Some time ago, I wrote another article about local Klan activities, and at that time, because of some of the material I had to draw from, I did name several names. In that case, individuals had taken out advertisements in a brochure published for a Klan rally and parade in 1924, and they signified their association with the Klan in any way they could. Local companies wrote that they were Kourteous, Klean, and Kareful, and one man advertised the Kellogg Keeps Kerosene. A year or two later, I met Kellogg's son—now a man in his eighties—and he said yes, he knew I had mentioned his father, and it was "okay" by him because it was all in the past.

Here is another situation. In the 1880s  a woman poisoned her two teen-age daughters, there was a court trial, and she was found guilty. In writing about the episode, do we use the woman's name? There is a business that carries that name in our town today. Would the present owner—who is no relation—mind? When I asked him, he said he did not think it would hurt him or his business, but he was glad that I mentioned it before it appeared in print.

What if there is a personal scandal or tragedy in a local family? Does the local historian have any use for such material? Being a fact of local history does not make a scandal itself anything to focus upon. It is only when facts and past events can be related to a larger picture that they deserve investigation and reporting. Certain people, by virtue of their position, lay open their lives to the public: the local historian often needs to deal with some of them.

What if, on the other hand, a scandal involved some betrayal of the public trust? What if the heir to the town's most respected family caused the family bank to fail? Here the personal scandal becomes part of a bigger picture, one that touches upon the loss of the financial institution to the community, and the consequences for those people in the town whose investments and trust had been placed in it. In that case, the failure of the bank places the family heir in the middle of the story. "I would not write the story of such a bank failure," said one local historian who had a similar episode in her community. But I think that I might. A bank failure is an important event. It affects the community, and it affects individuals. How the community reacts to it and how individuals cope are worthy issues to study. From such an investigation, we can learn a good deal.

Peggy Korsmo-Kennon, director of the Waseca County Historical Society, in Waseca, Minnesota, sent me an interesting problem concerning an individual's right to privacy. In a community history entitled *Blooming Prairie Update*,[6] written by Harold Severson and published in 1980, there was mention of a 1952 murder in the community. Writing some thirty years after the event, Severson noted that "few criminal trials have aroused greater interest" in Blooming Prairie. Severson wrote three paragraphs about the killing and then reprinted a contemporary account of the trial from the local newspaper. The material appeared in the middle of a long book. It is a topic that other local historians might include in a study of their area.

A problem arose, however, because the man convicted of the murder—which was an instance of domestic violence in which a police officer was killed—had served fourteen years in jail and was, in 1980, free. He had created a new life for himself in another community nearby. When the convicted murderer (whose name I am trying very hard not to use) read the piece about himself, he sued the publisher of the history, which happened to be the First National Bank of Blooming Prairie, and he sued the writer. The issue is complicated. None of us wants to cause others harm; but need we shy away from naming names, especially when the persons are still alive and the reason for their notoriety is unflattering? In a recent newspaper account of this whole issue, a University of Minnesota professor of law is quoted as saying that in regard to a criminal's right to privacy, "it's an awful murky area of law." He did note, however, that "it is very difficult for someone to win this kind of privacy suit unless the person can also show that some of the published information is false."[7]

The answer to the problem of privacy must be found in how material is used and for what purpose. In a general history, where the crime itself is not featured, the name of the individual is not really important. Severson got into trouble because he did not write the episode himself, giving it careful treatment and looking at the issue from some larger context. Instead, he simply reprinted the newspaper article directly into his history.

I am not qualified to give legal advice. But my historical common-sense advice would be this: if the story is important to the community history—perhaps because of the extreme forms of reaction on the part of the town—then the story can be written in such a way as to focus upon that community reaction, and not upon the individual involved. In other words, a bank failure is an important event, and so is a murder, and what they mean to a community is a legitimate focus to use. We do not want to heap more trouble upon the head of anyone, but someone convicted of a crime has surely lost his or her privacy where that issue is concerned. Being sensitive to the problem of people who have tried to make new lives for themselves, however, is decent behavior on our part. We are not judges, nor are we journalists.

Another example, handled differently: In some Ohio towns between 1866 and 1876, officials conducted a Board of Health survey that led to an examination of the premises of every home in the community. Each house was visited, the owner named, and the condition of the dwelling noted. This is potentially a very important piece of historical information: from it the historian could determine patterns of wealth, neighborhood patterns, and a good deal of information about the domestic life of the town. Writing about the survey, Helen Hooven Santmyer, author of *Ohio Town,* noted: "as for its scatological aspect — that in itself is material for pages of comment. It is a disillusioning subject, however, and best let alone."[8] The survey results sound like a rich strand of material, yet the historian herself has declared them out of bounds. She had, however, identified the material so that future historians can seek and use it.

In a number of ways, a community expects a good deal of its local historian. It expects breadth of interest from us, and it expects a degree of sensitivity to local attitudes. It expects that its history will be positive and that unflattering events from the past will not be hauled out in an accusatory fashion. It does expect the truth, but often the community is uncertain how much truth it can tolerate. I believe that if most communities had to select either the truth or a flattering biography, they would take their histories on the positive side. This is, of course, what has alway been given, and therefore the expectation that local history will be boosterish is built in.

A community takes for granted that local historians are interested in everything that happened and that we want to know about most things. We are expected to want to hear everyone's stories and to look at everyone's scrapbooks. This is sometimes the way we discover new material or meet interesting people; but it is also time-consuming and diverting, and sometimes we must assess our priorities in order to get our own work done. Unfortunately, such choices can be awkward for a newcomer if a long-time community historian has generally followed these more time-consuming practices. Each individual, however, must function in the way that he or she is most comfortable.

A community expects that the local historian will freely share what he or she knows about the local past. Most of us are willing to do so, but some requests go beyond what is possible and what can and should be expected of an individual. Some of these requests are discussed in the Coda to this chapter, and most local historians have other examples. The most exasperating request is the one from someone who wants to know "everything" about some aspect of community history "right away." Since I do not have in my head all the facts about my community, and since I do not want to pass on misinformation, my response to such encompassing requests is to tell the person where I would look to recover the information sought, but not to do the work for others myself. I always hope that someone intent upon a specific topic that involves him or her in community history will become so absorbed as to join the fray in earnest. Every researcher in the community is to be welcomed.

In states where there is no law controlling the disposition of public records (and probably in some states where such a law exists), communities have often left to local historians the care of public records. There are any number of cases where municipal records are even stored in the home of a local historian, so disinterested in them are many of our towns and villages. In Monroe County, New York, a local historian kept at his home all the extant town records — minute books, reports, lists of inhabitants, and the like. He also had his own extensive notes, taken over many years. Much of this material was filed, some stored in boxes, some piled on the floor. This system, while chaotic to an outsider and something of an eyesore to his family, made perfectly good sense to the local historian. All went well while the historian was alive, but when he died his family cleared out all the clutter. Loose papers were destroyed and the books and manuscripts sold to a local dealer. When the town fathers named a new municipal historian — New York state has a system of appointing local historians — she discovered the situation just as the dealer sold the collection. The Town Board made an attempt to recover the material, but it could do little more than receive permission that the collection be photocopied before it was dispersed. The collection of original documents was eventually scattered, and the originals of the town records no longer belong to the community.

Another story that illustrates this same point is one whose source I cannot track down. It concerns the history of the McGraw Free Central College, an interesting and curious institution that opened its doors in 1848 to students of both sexes and of any color. McGraw is a small central New York hamlet, located in Cortland County. It was believed to be close enough to the fine academies in Homer and Cortland to derive some good publicity from their existence. The college had been founded by anti-slavery Baptists; hence the "Free" in its name, which soon had to be changed because students arrived believing that there would be no fees. There were indeed some costs, although they were minimal, and students were credited for the manual labor required of everyone. The school became the New York Central College and flourished briefly until an outbreak of smallpox in 1850 caused the death of several students and generated local antagonism toward the institution. In addition, despite the number of abolitionists in central New York, there was a good deal of hostility to the actual mixture of the races. Finally, when a partially black instructor of ancient Greek married one of his white students, many people turned their backs on the college in the belief that mixing the races in classes encouraged intermarriage. Nearby newspapers viciously attacked the institution, money to run the school dwindled, and the state of New York refused to grant it a permanent charter. Despite backing by a number of noted liberals, by 1860 the college had disappeared.

Some years after the demise of the New York Central College, a historian appeared who wanted to record its history. He gathered together all the extant documents, took the note cards that he had amassed over the years concerning the college, and set out to an Adirondack hotel where he intended to write a book. The hotel, unfortunately, was wooden and old, and shortly after the historian checked in, it burned to the ground. The historian escaped, but all the documents detailing the college were lost. There are few sources left that tell of this interesting but short-lived institution.

❦

A historian in a nearby community contributes an additional story about the loss of documents. He reports that in his village for many years town meetings were held upstairs over a local hardware store. When town officials moved to new quarters, the old books and records were left behind in the attic. It was not believed that they were particularly useful documents, and no one gave them much thought. They had, after all, been safe in the hardware store for over one hundred years. A new owner of the hardware company, however, hired some local boys to remove the debris from the building, and during that cleanup they took the accumulated clutter to the town dump. There they poured gas on the old papers and set the pile afire. Town residents recall that for weeks afterwards scraps of burned ledger paper could be picked up along the main road.

These stories all originate in New York state, but New Yorkers are no more careless—or careful—of their public records than are residents of other states; and the twentieth century is no more guilty of disrespect and disdain for old materials than were people in other times. Dr. Thomas Addis Emmet in his autobiography, issued in 1911, tells an equally harrowing tale.[9] In medical practice during the Civil War, Dr. Emmet treated a patient who lived in Washington, D.C. She showed him letters dating from the post-Revolutionary era written by George Washington, Benjamin Franklin, and several other well-known individuals. The documents related to public service and surely belonged in government archives. The woman told Dr. Emmet that "on her way to the Capitol a few days before, she had to pass between a dozen or more tobacco hogsheads filled with papers so that they hung over the sides." The woman spied George Washington's name on a sheet of paper and asked a nearby workman if she might have it. She was told yes, "and that she might take as many as she wished as it was a lot of old rubbish which was to be destroyed."

Dr. Emmet inquired further and discovered that workmen were making room in the capitol for a bakery that was to supply bread to the nearby Union Army. The barrels containing government papers had been removed; they were considered of little use and were definitely in the way. The barrels were hauled into the alley where Dr. Emmet's patient found them, but they did not remain long in the street. One night a group of workmen took them and dumped the barrels and their contents into the Potomac River. Further inquiry proved that the barrels had been stuffed with official government papers during the administration of President James Madison, who had ordered that all government papers be stored in hogsheads. He insisted that every care be taken for their preservation so that the British, who were then advancing on the capital during the hectic days of the War of 1812, would not capture them. The documents survived the British threat but succumbed fifty years later during our own national emergency.

Records of national and local importance have in the past often fared poorly. Not only documents receive casual treatment; buildings, artifacts, maps, civil records, and odd pieces of the past that could be called ephemera have also suffered. Our national heritage is no longer in jeopardy, and local documents have recently gained a new degree of respect, yet the moral of these stories is that both documents and people are mortal. Our local records can never be safe when they are stored in a local historian's private dwelling, where they are in danger of being destroyed or of being considered part of the historian's personal possessions. Nor are documents safe when they are treated casually and carted about for use in inappropriate locations. And they cannot be considered safe until a community recognizes the heritage of the past and the importance of maintaining its records adequately. These public documents tell the stories of our communities: they belong to us all and to all ages. Many small towns and villages do not have any facilities for storage, and we all know of local historians who have saved documents by merely being willing to take over their care. In such a case, the local historian is to be commended. But that care should include pointing out to the municipality its responsibility to make provision for the records of its past. The community should be prevailed upon to buy a fire-proof cabinet or to create a small but protected archive for its records. Another solution would be for a locality to donate its papers to an existing local archive capable of undertaking their preservation. Any local historian who has possession of public records should insist that the town fathers find a safe and secure place where they can be kept.

Public documents are one thing, and the responsibility for their care is clear. What about those documents that are in private hands, private collections of historical materials? Most local historians collect whatever can be found about the area in which they live. We buy books when we can afford them, we pick up pamphlets, broadsides, posters, church bulletins, and many other types of materials that document our communities. Many of us also collect items that reflect the flavor of our own times. I know of a local historian who kept all the "junk" mail that came to her over the period of a year and then donated this pile of materials to a local historical society. At first, the society director was taken aback, not seeing the catalogues and announcements, political pamphlets, charity appeals, and trivia that reach most of us through our mailboxes as anything that the archive should acquire. Upon second thought, however, the society decided that these items reflected something important about our culture. They were boxed and shelved and put away for another era to exclaim over and learn from.

Most people now find the telephone "the next best thing to being there," and when they do receive a letter, it is usually quickly read and then tossed away. Ellen Goodman, the newspaper columnist, has written:

Sometimes I think that the telephone call is as earthbound as daily dialogue, while a letter is an exchange of gifts. On the telephone you talk; in a letter you tell. There is a pace to letter writing and reading that doesn't come from the telephone company but from our own inner rhythm. . . . There is leisure and emotional luxury in letter writing. There are no obvious silences to anxiously fill. There are no interruptions to brook. There are no nuances and tones of voice to distract. . . . A letter doesn't take us by surprise in the middle of dinner. . . . It waits. There is a private space between the give and the take for thinking. . . . How can you wrap a lifetime of phone calls in a rubber band for a summer's night when you want to remember?[10]

To hedge against leaving the next generation of historians with few personal documents, I began some years ago keeping all my correspondence. In addition to the material that simply came my way, I also generated a good deal of material by asking friends to write to me concerning episodes or events they had participated in or recalled. Over the years, I have received descriptions of the reactions of local people to the Viet Nam War and to the peace movement it spawned; to local environmental issues; to a major fire; remembrances of a flood and its consequences for the area; memoirs of Prohibition in our community; Depression stories; a tape-recorded letter from a member of our selective service board during the Second World War; and recollections of growing up and going to school in the area. My letters detail marital breakups and the subsequent strength shown by my women friends in plotting their own survival; they tell of birth, and of the dying of loved ones.

Usually when I ask someone to write to me about a local episode, I ask a specific question rather than one so sweeping in nature that the person does not know where to start. Instead of "Tell me about your life," or "Tell me all about politics in our city," questions that elicit either pages and pages of unfocused details or else a brief statement consisting of dates of major events, I try to ask a question about which my respondent can spin his or her own reactions and experiences. Instead of "Tell me about your life," I ask, "Did you see the high school the night it burned down?" or "Did you see any of the looting during the riots in the 1960s?" or "Who was you favorite schoolteacher, and what games did you play in the school yard?" These are broad enough questions to pull from the past both specific facts and a personal reaction. They are not so sweeping that a person does not know where to begin.[11]

In the same vein, a friend recently called to tell me that her mother was very ill and that she wanted to capture something of her mother's life on paper or tape so that her children might know her better. How should she go about it? There are, of course, good books that describe how to conduct an interview. These, however, are really intended for someone who is embarking on a major project rather than for a person who wants to talk with a family member to capture something of his or her past. My suggestion to my friend was to record her mother's life in the same way I suggest we gather community information. In what format would your mother be most comfortable responding, I asked—recorded sessions where you and the family talk with her or questions submitted for written answers? I recommended that she ask specific questions that would elicit both particular and general information and responses that would reflect her mother's opinions and reactions to events in her life. Every individual will have questions that are specifically appropriate for the individual; the general questions I suggested to my friend were these:
•the older generation: what did her mother remember of her grandparents and of their generation—who were they, where did they live, how did they make their living; what about their children, their home, holidays celebrated there; and some consideration of what being their grandchild meant.
•her parents' generation: the same questions could be asked of her parents along with specific questions that might be added about first car, Depression experiences, Prohibition memories, participation in miliary service, relationship with other siblings of their families, geographic mobility, education, aspirations, manner of handing out punishment, etc.
•school: what her mother recalled about her school days, subjects she enjoyed, teachers she liked and did not like, classmates, girls' clubs, preparations for the beginning of school—the shopping

trip for new clothes—parties, description of classroom, teachers' punishments of the unruly, school expeditions, etc.

•religious experiences: importance of religion to the family, attendance at religious classes and regular service, appearance of the church building, experiences with missionaries, attitudes about other religious groups, how other people felt about her religion, etc.

•growing up: major milestones recalled; music, art, sports lessons; first lipstick; things beyond bounds, such as places forbidden to her, people to be avoided; general fears and aspirations; menstruation; dating; courting; engagement; marriage; recollections of births of children; family vacations, etc.

•the community: places lived, what they looked like, services available, the library, community values, fearful places, places for family outings, picnics, cemetery visits, parks, old houses, community rituals such as Halloween practices, etc.

There are any number of other topics, depending upon the individual and the life he or she has led, and where that person has been. With these questions, my friend and her family spent many hours with her mother, and it was time that all of them considered to be rich and fulfilling. They learned a great deal about "grandma," much that revealed the essence of her character and values.

I prefer to gather my information in written form. I like asking questions that lead people to recall their lives and to describe their experiences. I like having the recollection written down for future use. And I like giving individuals the opportunity to reflect upon and reread their answers. Most often, for instance, when I have asked a specific question about a fight in a congregation concerning the demolition of an old building and the erection of a new one, I get a great deal more than a description of the arguments used by both sides. As a person becomes comfortable answering specific questions, he or she often moves beyond what is asked to spin out the account in a number of different ways. These digressions are often very useful, opening up subjects I knew little about and sometimes offering information I had not dared to ask about in the first place but was interested in knowing.

For some years, I have written to my friend Paul Bradford. Paul was born in my community more than eighty years ago. His mother was born here. His grandfather emigrated from England in the middle of the nineteenth century. Paul knows the city in which he has lived; he also knows ideas, words, events, and people from an era before his own. Often he can tell me what an old expression meant, and he has helped define several words for me. He failed with one phrase. I asked Paul if he knew what a "soiled dove" was. No. he replied. When I told him it was a newspaper term for a "lady of ill repute," he laughed and said he didn't know things like that! Paul is a skilled writer and seems to enjoy our correspondence. His letters are a vast treasure of information about our local past.

Letters of this sort are more than a private correspondence; they are part of the public memory, and they should not be destroyed. A number of people write to give me information, to offer a document for me to see and use, sometimes to correct me, or to ask questions about something they hope I will research. These letters are important too; all such correspondence is stored away in boxes marked with the name of a local archive destined to receive this material when I no longer am in need of it.

This, of course, brings up the issue of death and the local historian—for local historians do die. What should become of the collections that we all make—collections of a small but discrete nature as well as those that are far-ranging in topic and type? Should families dispose of this material? Not knowing what is of value and what archives might want, a family is often unable to make informed decisions about historical collections; yet a family is certainly justified in ridding the house of excess paper. Is this what local historians want for the material we have collected? And if tossing these papers out is not the proper course, then what should be done about a local historian's accumulation?

The answers to these questions can be rather simple; but because most of us do not care to think about a time when we might not be here, such considerations are usually put aside. Rare items from a collection should be set aside for donation or sale to a nearby archive. If a collection of books duplicates those found in the historical society, or in any other local archives, then there is no reason why a family should not sell them. A dealer should be sought who knows the value of such books and who has access to clients who are looking for local history materials. There are a good many sensitive antiquarian book dealers around the country.

Personal papers present a more complicated problem. Many scraps of paper in my study are notes to myself and are worthless to others. But filed away are copies of talks I have given; old copies of manuscripts, which, once published, are really of little value; some projects on which I embarked and for one reason or another abandoned; bibliographies for subjects that interested me; hints of projects that might be pursued and indications of where I might start such investigations. Materials of this sort should be offered to local archives. Not every historical society will want to keep such material, but some will, and they should be given an opportunity to receive it.

Failing that, what does one do with the historical "stuff" that we all gather? What should happen to all this material? My solution—and it is not one with which everyone will agree—is to name someone to whom this material will be passed. A younger local historian will get my files and bibliographies. I am therefore passing on to another historian some of the accumulation of the past as I have gathered and recorded it. That historian might learn some useful things and avoid some paths I have taken with no results. The chances are that some of what I have gathered together will be of help to another: to me this is the ideal solution to the problem of what we should do with our personal material. Passing materials on serves, just as donating a kidney or retina, to link one's life work to another's: a gift across time from one researcher in a community's past to another.

## NOTES

1. William Gilmore Simms, *Katharine Walton: or, The Rebel of Dorchester* (New York: Redfield, 1853), 2.

2. Johnny Farragher and Christine Stansell, "Women and Their Families on the Overland Trail, 1842-1867," *Feminist Studies* 2 (No. 2/3, 1975): 150-166; and Pierre-Jakez Helias, *The Horse of Pride* (New Haven: Yale University Press, 1978).

3. Marc Bloch, *The Historian's Craft* (Manchester, England: Manchester University Press, 1954), 44-45.

4. Theodore Zeldin, "Personal History and the History of the Emotions," *Journal of Social History* 15 (Spring 1982): 341-342.

5. A. F. C. Wallace, *Rockdale: The Growth of an American Village in the Early Industrial Revolution* (New York: Alfred A. Knopf, 1978).

6. Peggy Korsmo-Kennon to the author, 27 October 1981; *Minneapolis Tribune*, 22 October 1981, p. 4B; and Harold Severson, *Blooming Prairie Update* (Blooming Prairie, Minnesota: published as a community project by the First National Bank, Blooming Prairie, 1980), 233-234.

7. Dan Oberdorfer, "Community history stirs memories of '51 slaying in Blooming Prairie," *Minneapolis Tribune*, 22 October 1981, pp. 3B-4B.

8. Helen Hooven Santmyer, *Ohio Town: A Portrait of Xenia* (Columbus: Ohio State University Press, 1962; New York: Harper & Row, 1984), 90.

9. Dr. Thomas Addis Emmet, *Incidents of My Life* (New York: G. P. Putnam's Sons, 1911), 216.

10. Ellen Goodman, "Without Letters, Where are the Memories," *The Ithaca Journal*, 17 August 1985, p. 10.

11. See for example, William G. Hartley, *Preparing a Personal History* (Salt Lake City: Primer Publications, 1976); David E. Kyvig and Myron A. Marty, *Your Family History: A Handbook for Research and Writing* (Arlington Heights, Illinois: AHM Publishing Corporation, 1978); and David Weitzman, *My Backyard History Book* (Boston: Little, Brown and Company, 1975).

# Coda to Chapter Four:
## Telephone Calls

FOR SOME years, I have kept a list of the requests that come to me over the telephone. At first I did this because I wanted to keep track of the sorts of things the public wanted to know. Later, I decided such a list revealed something about the public's conception of who and what a local historian is. I have not listed the most common questions, those concerning architectural and genealogical information, which I usually turn over to the preservation or historical society. Nor have I listed those that are inquiries about giving talks or answering some specific question. An example of the latter might be a call from a school student who needs to know if there were three public hangings in our community or four (the answer is three). My calls are similar to those every local historian receives, although my list contains a number of requests from graduate students at a nearby university—students who for a variety of reasons decide to write M.A. dissertations on subjects that touch upon our local past.

This, then, is an edited and partial list:

•A third-grade teacher called to ask me to spend two hours with one of her students, and his parents, in order to tell them all I knew about one of the benefactors of our community.

•A grade-school teacher investigating local history for the first time called to request that I tell her "everything."

•A graduate student called wanting names of old people in the community who could be interviewed for a twenty-minute-long videotape program she planned to present to high-school students.

•A graduate student asked for information about local inns, taverns, and hotels, from the first in the area to those presently serving travelers.

145

•A friend called to ask for a "good" topic for her son's seventh-grade local history project.

•A professional writer asked for information for an article she was preparing.

•A woman producing a local pageant called to ask me to tell her all the local folk tales I could recall for use in her play.

•An elderly woman called to tell me of her ability to find three, four, and six-leaf clovers, every month of the year. She does not pick five-leaf clovers because they are bad luck.

•A woman cleaning out her attic called to ask if I wanted to come by to see if there was anything of interest.

•A friend called to ask if I could insert local history publicity in the newspaper in which my weekly local history articles appear.

•A schoolboy called to ask for dates of columns I had written several years ago concerning a local park.

•A woman from an adjoining county asked what I knew about a particular school district in her county. She insisted that I must know. (I didn't.)

•A woman called who owns a friendship quilt on which there are over one hundred names. Would I come look at the quilt and identify the people who stitched on their names?

•A representative of a local park called to ask how log cabins in our area were built.

•A man called to discuss his interest in the Civil War with me.

•An elderly man called to invite me to join him in a cave he knows about if we are ever faced with a nuclear war. He thought his ingenuity and my knowledge of the local past would make us the best candidates for survival.

•A school librarian called to ask me to explain the difference between various aspects of the new state-mandated social studies curriculum so she would know with which grade certain books should be put.

•An elderly, blind woman called to share with me her memories of growing up in the area.

In all, they were an interesting (and sometimes amusing) batch of callers. Some of the calls I followed up on: I went to see the lady's attic treasures, I suggested several topics to my friend for her son, I talked a long while with the woman about her memoirs, I thanked the man with the cave and told him I would do my best to work for nuclear disarmament. I discussed the problem of books and curriculum with the librarian, and I followed up on the interesting folklore about multi-leaf clovers.

I told the teacher to have her student and his parents read a biography of the man they were interested in and then to call me if they had any questions. The boy called some time later, and we discussed his interest.

I gave out the dates of my articles about the creation of a local park, and I gave my friend advice about publicity. I encouraged the woman with the quilt to copy from it all the information she could and then to see if the signers might have been in a club or church group with her parents, or if they might have been neighbors. She eventually worked out the information that interested her.

The difficult calls were those from people who were genuinely interested in learning more about local history but who wanted me to tell them all I knew. In the first place, that is an impossible task not because I, or any other local historian, knows so much, but because "all" is so unfocused a request that it leads one nowhere. To callers who ask for great segments of knowledge, I usually give a list of the places in which I would look for that information. In other words, if they are interested, then I give them the means to follow up their interest on their own. I am always willing to answer questions, but I hope that by immersing others in our history, they too will become interested researchers.

In addition, I distrust my own memory, and I like to have things written down in order to get them right. To talk about a topic about which I am unfamiliar, I would have to research it. It is better that the individual with the interest or need conduct his or her own investigation. Obviously, if the caller is someone unable to pursue the research, I do my best to help focus the questions and then to answer them. I am always willing to discuss causes, and reasons, and results with such people, and I encourage them to call back after they have done some research, so that we can talk about what they have discovered. This seems to be a reasonable way of dealing with people: fair to them, and fair to myself.

# 5 🐾 Writing Local History in the Popular Press

*An amateur because he loves things, may in the course of his life,
find points at which to dig deep.*

JACOB BURCKHARDT (1869)[1]

SOME OF the liveliest local history being written today appears in our hometown newspapers. Nonetheless, it is a neglected form of local history. No one writes about it and few people comment upon it. The neglect is not new. *The Newspaper and the Historian*, published in 1923, includes no discussion of the press as a place in which to publish local history. One article, dating from 1932, deals with the relationship between local history and newspapers. Its author delves into various aspects of the relationship between local historians and the press, but he regards newspapers only as a *source* of material for the historian rather than as a place in which to publish local history. Indeed, in his opinion, historical material cannot sufficiently interest readers to warrant its being carried in a newspaper.[2]

Nothing could be further from the truth. Local history has long had an important place in the popular press, and it is alive and well there today. In fact, of all the forms of written local history that there are—books, pamphlets, pieces in scholarly journals and those in magazines of history that are not so weighty, exhibition catalogues, and historical agency newsletters—there is probably no type of local history that is read as widely as those articles that appear in our local, hometown newspapers.

Newspapers reach large numbers of people who would never buy a book of local history, visit a historical society, or subscribe to a journal of history. When history pieces appear in a familiar medium, however, they are accessible to a great many people who are tempted to read them because they are about people and events of the locality, because they are short, and because they are often illustrated with beguiling old-time pictures. I do not want to claim that every newspaper subscriber reads the local history items—all newspaper readers do not read the sports pages—but many do, and I am always pleasantly surprised when someone unexpectedly mentions one of my articles.

To last any time at all in a newspaper, a series on local history must be interesting to the editor and to the public. One city editor reminded me recently that a newspaper is not an educational organ, but "a business." Of greatest importance to the people who run newspapers are articles that attract and maintain readers, or pieces that help make the paper attractive to advertisers. Poorly written or dull series on local history will last no time at all.

Local history is viewed by some editors as providing the right sort of local touch. In fact, in my search for local history columns around the country, I have found a few written by editors themselves. Such history articles provide a positive local focus in newspapers harried by costs, upstaged by television news coverage, and forced in many cases to rely upon sensational headlines to sell papers.

Local history articles have appeared in newspapers for a long time. Generally, local newspapers produced some of their first articles about local history after a community was established but before the death of all of the earliest pioneers. These articles were often in the form of reminiscences. Sometimes a paper printed documents with the explanation that the item was in danger of being lost or forgotten, or that it faced possible disintegration. This early impetus for articles of local history was most often commemorative: the anniversary of a town's founding, the origin of a local business, or the centennial of a religious institution often resulted in a special issue or section recalling its history. The destruction of a landmark building might have inspired reminiscent articles even before historical preservation became a community byword. In general, these early columns were written by members of the newspaper staff, although on some occasions a community member volunteered to solicit memoirs of the settling generation.

In the 1930s, local history came into its own in the popular press. The format changed, from reprints of documents and interviews with old-timers to history as feature story, or grist for an ongoing column, often with a by-line, that reported on the facts and fancies of a locality. In such cases, local history became associated with an individual who was known to be responsive to local rhythms and who published his or her findings on a regular basis. The local historical society was often viewed as one of many sources for the writer, but it was the opinion of many people, and most especially of the writers themselves, that it took their talent to translate the documents and the oral tradition into something palatable for the public.

As a number of journalists seized upon the stuff of local history as the basis of regular signed columns, these writers brought with them the training of their profession. Their dedication was less to Clio than to entertaining readers—and to pleasing editors. Some of them took literary license to "improve" a story or to insure a punch line. They were influenced by the folklorists and regional-color writers of their day, whose material was interesting and appeared to be simple to collect and write. These journalists of the 1930s, and onward, interviewed people for a knowledge of place, and they produced well-crafted pieces of local color, based primarily upon oral testimony. Often they specialized in reproducing an approximation of a local dialect and in using familiar local sayings. Their writings were extremely popular with the public. Their popularity meant that, for most people, they interpreted local history to the community.

It is difficult to fault these writers. They never set themselves up to be historians, even if the public regarded them as such. Yet their goal, as stated by one such author, was to turn history around. Historians, said Henry Charlton Beck of New Jersey, stressed the big things and the big places and have "ignored. . . the little things and places without which the canvas could not be complete." Beck insisted that his history was full of life; he was impatient with the dry-as-dust school of local historians or antiquarians, who would accept "nothing until every *i* is dotted, every *t* crossed, and every detail run to earth no matter what its significance."[3] And to be fair, the works of these writers were far more interesting to read than were many of the books of local history being produced.

Beck's critics claimed that he absorbed material and used it up in great quantities. They claimed he rushed into print without thorough investigation. He was careless, they said, about getting names and details straight; he accepted long-discarded versions of episodes; he talked with the wrong people or with people who knew only one side of the story. His emphasis was often suspect. He generalized too freely. All this, and even more, is true of Beck and his newspaper colleagues. Yet Beck's writings were so widely popular with the reading public that thirty years after original publication, his books are still being reprinted—some by a university press.

These criticisms are important to note, even though many of them can be explained away. They reveal Beck as a writer—and a clever one—who wrote up his material as it was gathered and who worked under the pressure of meeting weekly deadlines. Yet once something appears in print, as we all know, it gains a cachet of legitimacy and takes on a life of its own. The local historians who complained about Beck were those people determined to set the record straight.

Beck and other writers like him used stories long discredited chiefly because they did most of their research in the field, not in the library. Beck was not a historian interested in keeping up with the latest interpretation of the past; he was a collector who siphoned off from whomever he encountered whatever they knew. He took the material that came to hand and was satisfied to fashion that into an article; he had no need—even if we think he should have had that need—to verify his material. I am sure Beck would have said that, if someone believed something, that made it worthy of being collected and written, even if that item was not true in itself. His was a folklore approach to gathering knowledge without bothering with folkloric method and system. Had Beck and his contemporaries looked for balanced views of the stories they reprinted, they might have spoiled the effect of the anecdotes they were intent upon telling. A woman once complained to me that she had attempted to correct something one of these writers had published in a local paper. The writer's version was incorrect, and this woman has a passion for putting the record straight. After explaining the accurate version to the writer, she expected that there would be a correction and was shocked to hear: "It sounds better that way!"[4]

The journalists who became involved with local history used historical data. They often failed to find out the context of the stories they unearthed. Their pieces appeared in the press because they were well written and lively; they were often accepted as local history; and they became examples of what local history should be.

There are a great many people writing local history articles in newspapers today. A few are journalists; many are independent local historians; some are representatives of local historical societies; and a number are college professors who have turned to local history as an aspect of what they teach.

In an attempt to find out what local history is being presented to the public in newspapers, I advertised my interest in *History News*, the magazine of the American Association for State and Local History. I received a number of responses, many from people who thoughtfully answered my questions, all of whom sent copies of their articles. In talking about writing local history in newspapers, then, I will draw from my own experience and also from the comments of the people who have corresponded with me. This is in no way a comprehensive look at local history writing today in newspapers, but it is representative.

Local history is alive and well represented in the newspapers of our hometowns, in American small town papers. Some columns, I learned, were of long standing, but a great many began during or after the Bicentennial. They are written all across the country and the names of some of those I have discovered appear below:


"Nostalgia"                    *Harvard* (Illinois) *Herald*
"California Vignettes"         *Vallejo Independent Press*
"Pages from the Past"          *Vallejo* (California) *Times Herald*
"Window on the Past"           *The Sunday Oklahoman* (Geary,
                               Oklahoma)
"Yesteryears"                  *San Angelo* (Texas)
                               *Standard-Times*
"Historical Moments"           *Lassen County Times* (Susanville,
                               California)
"Historically Speaking"        *North Haven* (Connecticut) *Post*
"What a Week it Was"           *Milwaukee* (Wisconsin) *Journal*
"Remember When"                *Milwaukee Journal*
"New Stories from Old          *Lafayette* (Indiana) *Journal and*
    Lafayette"                 *Courier*
"99 Years Ago"                 *Noble County American*
                               (Albion, Indiana)
"Of Local Interest"            *The Review* (Baldwinsville, New
                               York)
"West Bluff Streets"           *West Bluff Word* (Peoria, Illinois)
"From the Antiquarian          *Daily Times and Chronicle*
    Society Notebook"          (Reading, Massachusetts)
"Smoky Valley Roots"           *Salina* (Kansas) *Journal*
"Focus"                        *The Times Argus* (Barre-
                               Montpelier, Vermont)
"Posey County Pioneers"        *Posey County* (Indiana) *News*
"Loose Nuggets"                *Anchorage* (Alaska) *Daily News*
"The Way We Were"              *Chicago Tribune*


Some columns have changed names over time, sometimes indicating that a new writer has taken over, other times indicating a shift in the focus of the column. "Geary Glimpses," which appeared in the *Junction City Republic* (a weekly) and in *The Union* (a daily paper), both published in Junction City, Kansas, became the "Curator's Corner" when the Geary County Historical Society took it over. As "Glimpses," the column was written by a local couple, containing a blend of "95% historical with 5% museum announcements." Now that a historical society employee is writing the column, "about 50% of column space" is devoted to information about displays, new acquisitions, and special programs at the society.

My own column began as "Pieces of the Past," but my editors — looking in vain for something catchy — renamed it "History," and so it has been for at least six years. My predecessor at the newspaper wrote under the title of "Glance Backwards." The names of these local history articles identify the column as something from the local past, not the whole story but a segment of it. Most of the columns I have come across have been intended for one newspaper, and the geographic area served tended to be one county.

In the responses to my request for information about local history columns, however, there were two cases where articles were written to serve a broader community than a single county. This is an appealing way of getting history to the public and of using an article efficiently. Stuart Sprague, professor of history at Morehead State University, in Morehead, Kentucky, wrote to tell me of his series, "Kentucky Yesterdays," articles intended to cover a twenty-county area of the state. Sprague reported that he "used the college's public information service as a delivery system," to distribute the column and to generate good will for the college. He selected topics that were at the local (county) level "or ones that would interest the entire region." While not every newspaper used Sprague's articles, many in the area did and were enthusiastic about them. Sprague used a Kentucky Humanities Council grant to travel to archives in order to prepare his material, and he also assigned his students papers on local topics. Another individual who set out to write a history column for a broader audience is Philip Roberts, senior historian at the Wyoming State Archives, Museums, and Historical Department. Roberts reports that "in 1978 I originated what has become a very popular column in Wyoming newspapers. Called 'Buffalo Bones—Stories from Wyoming's Past,' the column is mailed to all newspapers in the state twice a month." Roberts reports that between twenty-five and thirty newspapers use the column regularly, and others pick it up on occasion.

When Roberts began, he envisioned "Buffalo Bones" being written by a number of different individuals from his state office, but for two years he alone produced articles, while the others cautioned, "It will never fly." When, at the end of the second year, Roberts compiled previous columns in a small book, his colleagues became interested, and since then they have contributed eagerly to the effort.

However it is produced, a regular column in a newspaper is good publicity for history. Tim Purdy, of Susanville, California, noted that his column, "Historical Moments," is "the most popular feature in the *Lassen County Times*. This is partly due to the fact that this [is] a rural mountain region where many descendants of the first settlers still reside." Other writers have noted that they believe their articles were favored by older readers and have been pleasantly surprised that younger people have found them interesting, too. Phil Roberts began producing "Buffalo Bones" because Wyoming had experienced a tremendous population increase in the last decade and the newcomers had little knowledge of the state's rich past. "What we have found," he noted, is that while newcomers enjoy the articles, it is the "long-time residents [who] are among our most loyal readers."

According to Miriam A. Barclay, secretary of the Reading Antiquarian Society in Reading, Massachusetts, the column in the *Daily Times and Chronicle* is considered an important outreach program of the society. Barclay noted that she knew the pieces were read, but was disappointed "that it has not done much to increase our membership." Others noted benefits they derived from writing. There is a joy in people's awareness of history being heightened, noted Lucy Brusic of North Haven, Connecticut, who commented—as did others — that the discipline of writing a weekly column sharpened her writing skills.

William Snell, professor of history at Lee College, in Cleveland, Tennessee, writes a column entitled "At a Snell's Pace" for his local paper. He views his articles as an "opportunity to share the historical heritage of the community with the reading public and also to solicit information (documents, photographs)" from them. A number of people noted that as columnists they receive a good deal of information, a number of suggestions for future articles, and often letters requesting further information. Irving Weber of Iowa City commented that he enjoys "recording the history of the city, the county, and the University. I have a big following and get countless phones calls. It has been a great hobby, and I drifted into it, thinking I would do about 20, and then the project grew and grew."

Others began columns because of an interest in genealogy. Judy Lilly of Salina, Kansas, noted she is a "housewife and mother who has a passion for genealogy and history with an added desire to write. Four years ago I approached the *Journal* about a history column with space for genealogical queries. The editors were receptive, and the paper has been printing 'Smoky Valley Roots' regularly, ever since."

Robert Kiebel, editor of the *Journal and Courier* of Lafayette, Indiana, writes a weekly local history column. He wrote: "My goals in writing about local history are to give readers something interesting and unusual to read each week, to educate, explain and entertain. A readership survey conducted in 1980 indicated the column had a substantial following."

Writers of history articles for newspapers encounter some common problems. Few complain about the amount of space allotted to history columns, but it is generally limited. Some columns are as short as 200 words, with 750 words or under three typed pages, double spaced, the average length. A few columns are limited to a caption beneath an interesting old photograph.

The research for these columns, on the other hand, can be staggering: one writer estimated that he spent thirty hours on each essay. This time is not really compensated by money. Writers noted (in

1983) that they were paid nothing, or they received a copy of the newspaper, or they got three dollars a column and two for each picture printed, on up to fifty dollars per week, which is just about tops for a writer who only submits a history column and is not on the newspaper staff in any other capacity.

Another problem is that of authenticating what we have written — or the question of footnotes. Landa Hammond, director of education at the Oswego (New York) Historical Society, which submits a weekly history column to a nearby newspaper, noted that the columns produced each week go to the paper with footnotes attached. The paper, however, does not use the notes. As a backup, the society keeps a copy, which contains the documentation, of each article it sends to the paper. When the story appears, it is clipped and filed with the typed manuscript copy. In this way, the historical society has a complete file of articles as they were written, and as they appeared in the paper; footnotes are kept with the printed version to provide documentation, if needed. Writers working alone can proceed in the same fashion, keeping original footnoted copies of stories sent to the newspaper. Articles can also be footnoted in the "sneaky" fashion described on page 102, or they can be annotated after they appear in the press by making notations of sources to be filed with the printed copies. In these ways, we make an attempt to give credit to our sources and to let those who come after us know how we know.

Most writers practice a sort of self-censorship. Irving Weber noted: "I write only happy things: no old time murders, or scandals. If someone asks me to leave something out, I observe their wishes; so [I] am not a good reporter. Once in awhile I have to leave out something that would add to a story. But I have to live with these people. They are my friends." And so do we all, so the question of what to include and what to omit is particularly important.

Lucy Brusic put the situation this way: "The problem in writing history for newspapers is that good history and good newspaper copy are not always identical or coincident. I sometimes felt that I was either a little dry (in order to get in all the facts) or a little 'flip' (to make good reading)." We do walk a fine line. We want the exposure for our material that a newspaper provides, while at the same time we are not journalists, but historians.

I have encountered criticism of something I wrote, and for reasons that illustrate another sort of problem. In a long piece about women from our area who had gone to nurse during the Civil War, I quoted Walt Whitman. As you know, there was strong public sentiment against women going off to war, and army doctors regarded nurses with something less than enthusiasm. Whitman, too, had reservations about white women nursing soldiers. He wrote: "There are plenty of excellent clean old black women that would make tip-top nurses." A few days after the column appeared, I received a phone call from a reader who complained that I had no right printing such a racist statement. I attempted to point out that I had not written the sentence in question but had quoted Walt Whitman, who was speaking as many of his generation did about blacks. In fact, Whitman, it seems to me, showed a particularly fine sensitivity, for harsher and meaner words describing blacks in the 1860s were in common use. My caller would not be convinced. Here, we have an instance of a 1980's sensibility regarding racial epithets being applied to an 1860's situation. Whitman's words were right to use, and his quotation was an important part of the story to be told.

A similar situation occurred after I published a long article concerning the treatment of Irish Roman Catholics, who came into my community in the 1840s and 1850s. My point was not that the Irish were unruly but that when an Irish man or woman was brought before the court he or she was identified as being Irish, while others were called only by their names, or protected by being charged as "John Does." Most of the cases that required the attention of a judge involved drinking and brawling. This article was part of an ongoing study of ethnicity in my community, about the reactions of those in place to newcomers, of nativism, and of the process of becoming an accepted part of society. The treatment accorded to the Irish was little different from the treatment the Irish accorded others who came at the end of the century when the Irish were comfortably placed.

One reader responded to this material in a strong fashion, suggesting that all the column that Saturday was good for was to wrap the garbage. The reader believed local history should only be complimentary and not expose our foibles in times past.

To only write "the good things" is to set the past up as the "good old days," suggesting that nothing since then has measured up. Yet the incident with the Walt Whitman quotation proves just the opposite: things have in many instances gotten better, the past was not a bucolic time of peace and plenty, there were mistakes and fools then just as there are now. What history can show is that prejudices we have managed to shed were commonplace in another era.

This brings up the subject of subjects for newspaper articles. Due to the lack of space, whatever is presented must be brief. I often run a series if I have more material than will fit in one week's offering, and other people do the same. When doing so, however, some sort of recap of the previous installment is usually necessary not because people missed the earlier segment but because it is easy to forget, one week to another, just what was being discussed.

Topics are endless, in number and kind. A newspaper is a good place to show the careful use of a document; a letter perhaps, or diary extracts on a single topic such as Christmas preparations, the Fourth of July, engagements, a local disaster. In fact, disasters are among the most popular subjects, and often a disaster article will pick up readers who are not faithful to the column. Census material can be used in a newspaper column, especially if the focus is on a topic like occupations revealed in a particular year, or reasons for decline or growth in overall population figures. Many people review books of local history in their columns, ranging around the state or region to pick up interesting materials their local readers might otherwise miss.

Seasonal topics are also popular, from celebrations such as Halloween and Thanksgiving to election episodes around Election Day and local traditions associated with particular times of the year.

The newspaper is a good place to look at the lives of local individuals who have in some way made their mark. It is also a fine forum for investigations of architectural trends, the literary history of a community, education history, and changes in the natural and the built environment. Local folklore is always appealing to the public, and it often generates letters giving variations and even new forms. Kent Ruth, of Geary, Oklahoma, noted, "I get best response from old picture contests, one room school memories." Many others agree.

On occasion, I use local history papers created by students at our community college or the works of students in seventh-grade local history class. In every case where I use other people's material, if it is documents that I have turned into an article or submissions by students or others, I make sure that the individual who has aided the column that week receives credit.

Other times, I attempt to answer questions I have been asked by readers. Sometimes I present a story that is only half done in hopes of learning more. I also try to feature local history created by other people, from note cards with local scenes to books and articles concerning our area. In a long series explaining all the historical markers in our county, I bemoaned the fact that some that were in place were frivolous, while others that should have been erected never were. Travelers' accounts of an area are usually popular, but so too are stories of local murders (those from the nineteenth century) and sensational court trials.

In other words, I use almost all phases of our past. Some articles I handle with extra care, so that old events are not used to create new wounds. I try always to be fair, and I try to be honest. I write what I believe to be true — in every case, but one. That one instance concerns reviewing local history books, for here one is judging one's peers, and one's neighbors, and here, I find, I shade my own opinions somewhat. My solution to the problem of reviewing a local history book is to describe the contents and not comment upon the historical method, the grammatical constructions, or the way the subject has been handled.

❦

I am often asked: How does one get started writing a local history column? A great number of people believe in the direct approach; if there is no history column in a local paper, the best tack is to write three or four short articles and make an appointment with the editor. Show the editor what you can do, ask for suggestions on ways in which changes could be made to suit the style of the press, and be prepared with a list of future topics you are interested in tackling. In this way, the editor can see what you are capable of writing, and a judgment can be made concerning inclusion in the paper. Stuart Sprague noted that when an editor is reluctant to use local history material, he writes an article about the development of the press in that person's town. Editors, it seems, are interested in the history of journalism; if their papers are featured, they often rise to the bait.

Other writers suggest that pictures are essential to any article about local history. If you have a source of good pictures, such as a historical society archive, you might work in tandem to prepare illustrated articles—giving credit to the society archive. Some writers take modern photos to accompany their articles, some use a combination of old and new images. Pictures are popular both with the public and with newspapers.

And so are quizzes. Dale Stirling, historian with the Department of Natural Resources in the state of Alaska, noted that the "'Great Alaska History Quiz' was fun to compile and it was received well by the community—particularly in the schools and the nearby university." This type of article has great appeal and has "a challenge factor. In other words, it's not stuffy academic stuff!" The full-page quiz, which appeared in the *Anchorage Daily News*, contained multiple-choice questions, picture questions, true or false, and questions that required the reader to fill in the blanks. The scoring for the fifty-question quiz went like this:

> 1-10 correct: You're still a cheechako [a newcomer].
> 10-20 correct: Better, but no sourdough yet.
> 20-30 correct: You know more about Alaska than you thought.
> 30-40 correct: You're qualified to teach high school Alaska history.
> 40-50 correct: You're now qualified to teach Alaska history at the University of Alaska.

The one danger with quizzes is that they are often suggestive. In writing a question, we do not want to set up a wrong idea or confirm a general—but incorrect—impression in print. If the Little Rascals never came to your community to make a film, even though many people believe that they might have, you ask for trouble if you write a true/false question asking if the Little Rascals came to town. Even if you indicate the incorrectness of this belief, little has been done to eradicate it from the public lore. Writing quiz questions should be done with care.

At a seminar I led on the topic of writing local history in hometown newspapers, a man said that he gone to his local editor with several articles in hand, each nicely illustrated, and had requested that space be given to a local history series. It was during the Bicentennial, and local history was hard to resist, but this editor was uninterested. The man said that he would provide the articles for free, if the paper was unwilling to pay him for them. Still, the editor was unmoved.

"What did you do?" I asked.

"Oh," he laughed, "I bought the paper!"

This is certainly one way of getting local history articles before the public, although it might not be within the means of every local historian.

Once the idea of a column has been accepted by a newspaper, find out how you can best meet its format. Articles should be typed, double spaced. Pictures should carry credit lines and caption information. Your identification should be noted; if the article is being sponsored by the local historical society, credit should be given to the society and to the person who actually wrote the piece. A column is most successful if it appears each week in the same place in the paper, and generally with the same format. Observe deadlines; most newspapers would prefer that material such as local history, which does not have to be used immediately, be submitted a week or two in advance. My practice is to be three weeks ahead with my columns, which gives the newspaper lead time in preparing the articles and allows me to function without a deadline always present.

🐟

Most of the historians from whom I heard mentioned that they wanted to bring out a book containing their best columns, and several mentioned that they had already done so. The desire to preserve carefully written history articles is strong; I hate to think of all the work involved in writing them "wasted" because newspaper articles seem ephemeral. Some historians collect their material, bind it, and submit it to a library or archive for preservation. Others seek publishers for it. Most commercial presses are uninterested in these collections because, as one editor said to me, "They really do not add up to a book." This attitude, happily, is not shared by the public at large, who often respond favorably to a new volume of local history, and many small presses are anxious to pick up local material to increase their backlists.

Often books of collected articles are privately published, or are sponsored by a historical society or some booster organization in the community that sells the volume and makes some money in the process. Few authors benefit financially from the publication of their material, although some people claim differently.

Looking at books of local history articles from other places can give us ideas useful in our own locales with our own material. Often such books suggest new topics and new ways of dealing with a weekly column. It is surprising how interesting other people's history can be to us — especially when it is well written and sprightly. Too few of us bother to read it. If you are in Wyoming, look up "Buffalo Bones." It is a fine example of local history writing in the public press.

🐟

Writing local history in newspapers requires that the historian view his or her material in small bits. The writing needs to be lively, and pictures should be included wherever possible. Topics should range about the history of the area, not only in time but in subject and kind. Newspaper writing puts local history in the hands of a great number of people, and their response is important. Often they have additional comments; sometimes they have suggestions for new topics to investigate; frequently they come up with material that has long been hidden or forgotten. The direct communication between the writer and reader is closer when you write for a newspaper than when you publish books or magazine articles. The reader is more likely to comment on the article, whether pleasing or displeasing, and that local response is gratifying to a writer. Because the pieces to be used are short, writing itself can be an easier process than it might be in a long project. Writing regularly and frequently is the best means to improve writing skills—an added benefit.

The problems of preparing a newspaper history column are few but important to note. They include using names and events of recent vintage; pleasing editors while at the same time being true to your material and to historical inquiry; limited space (usually only conquered by running series rather than cramming everything into four pages or less); and the fact that the work results in little or no pay. One of the joys, however—as Gwendolyn Danner, an Illinois writer, noted—is that "sometimes I feel better acquainted with the people who lived in Harvard before I was born, than I do with the ones I see every day—certainly, I know more about them."

A weekly column can be a potent vehicle. The local historian identified with such a series will take on the mantle of an authority. Questions and materials will be directed to him or her. A timely column can have a good deal of impact upon a community, and that responsibility should not be taken lightly. When a historic church is threatened by demolition because its congregation wants something modern, an article about the history of the building can make a difference (or exacerbate a split in the church or community). A school-board fight might elicit an article about an earlier dispute that is apt to put the current battle in some sort of perspective. A dirty election trick might bring forth a history article about earlier "dirty tricks"; in the case of my community, a political hoax was played in the 1844 presidential election that gave the name "Roorback" to such antics. A column about diversity at a time of racial or religious tension can help a community see itself in new ways. We should be conscious of the power of the press, and the power of the printed word—a power even local historians can enjoy when writing for our hometown newspapers.

## NOTES

1. Jacob Burckhardt, *Reflections on History* (1943; Indianapolis: Liberty Classics, 1979), 54.

2. Lucy M. Salmon, *The Newspaper and the Historian* (New York: Oxford University Press, 1923); and Carl L. Weicht, "The Local Historian and the Newspaper," *Minnesota History* 13 (March 1932): 45-50.

3. Henry Charlton Beck, *More Forgotten Towns of Southern New Jersey* (Rahway, New Jersey: Quinn & Boden, 1963), 5-6.

# 6 🐚 *Local History Today and Tomorrow*

*. . . there are wise historians among the amateurs of local history and dull gleaners of facts among the renowned professors of the universities.*

JOHAN HUIZINGA (1929)[1]

THE APPEAL of local history is universal, and local histories can be found worldwide. One look at the card catalogue of any major library reveals local history studies from communities scattered about the globe. In some places, local historians practice independently; in others, a district or the state takes an active role in supporting local history activities. The examples of these other forms that local history may take can be illuminating to the practice of local history in our own country.

In Norway, local history was once diverse, and individuals wrote of their home places as the story pleased them, without theme or direction. In the 1940s, however, Andreas Holmsen of Oslo University turned his hand to the study of local history, and he devised a way of proceeding that has dominated local history writing in that country ever since. Holmsen constructed a chronological outline of the history of Norway, from settlement to modern times. That became the framework for his study. Then, because of the rural nature of life in Norway outside its few major cities, Holmsen decided that local history should consider a locality through its farms. Thus Norwegian local history came to be known as *bygdebok*. A *bygd* is a small rural district, and so the first part of the word denoted that a local historian looks at the district; *bok* is the word for farm, indicating that each farm within the *bygd* was studied.[2] To keep local researchers informed about local history, and to connect them with new historical advances, there is a Norwegian local studies journal.

In Finland, local history is known as *kotiseutuyo*, or home-district work. Here local history is combined with ethnology, the development of communities, and ecological studies, and it is practiced in Finland's districts. There is a home-district federation that develops studies of culture in localities, supports the preservation of special features, influences social planning, awakens interest in the area, supports local enterprise, publishes material about the district, organizes training, gives advice, and works with other local organizations.[3] This is a more activist and comprehensive approach to local history than that taken by most historical societies in the United States: *kotiseutuyo* sounds rather like a combination of preservation society, historical and environmental association, chamber of commerce, and municipal planning department.

Local history can also be found throughout the Orient. In Japan, local histories are usually chronicles commissioned by a village mayor or official. A few of these histories are written by individuals who simply decide to relate an area's past; some are written by academics. There is also a tradition in Japan of well-regarded amateurs whose specialty is the writing of community histories. These people are frequently brought in to produce a town or village history. Local history is often undertaken in a school, sometimes by one class. Students compile historical data that will be shaped into a history, or a part of a history, and it will be published locally. There seems to be, in Japan, a strong concern about community history, and feelings run high about the history of one's native place. To the Japanese, a locality is "a significant part of their individual identities."[4]

A Japanese local history can be a vast undertaking, beginning with a discussion of the geology of the area, a description of the prehistoric peoples who inhabited what is now the village, and a narrative of events and changes that have occurred there. Keith Brown, who has translated a Japanese local history into English, notes in his introduction to *Shinjo: The Chronicle of a Japanese Village* that most Japanese local histories rarely attempt to generalize about what the events and changes under discussion mean for the nation or the society as a whole. Such a history, however, provides a vast amount of information, including, in Shinjo, a list of rice prices for the 123 years from 1830 to 1952.[5]

Local studies are also popular in China. In a study of local history, Meng-bai Zhang, of Suzhou University, states that among the ancient books still extant, of which there are some one hundred thousand titles, one-tenth of them are *fang zhi*, or local studies. *Fang* represents the Chinese character meaning local, or referring to a definite area, and *zhi* is the character used to represent the idea of record or register. Zhang estimates that the earliest *fang zhi* date to the Warring States Period, or to a time over 2,000 years ago. One emperor even employed an official historian to write down all the important events during the years of his reign, and regional princes and lesser administrators followed suit. Much of the early Chinese local history had its origin in geographical studies and maps; defending and maintaining territory in ancient China was a necessary occupation.

Zhang notes that Chinese histories had five common traits. They were records rich in local color, designed to reflect the particular features of a clearly defined region; they stressed continuity; they were encyclopedic in scope, being systematic records of an area; they were based on the idea that they would record happenings, but not comment upon them; and lastly, because they were most often generated by a local governmental unit, they were considered to be reliable documents. These histories were not without their flaws, but they have nonetheless been very useful to Chinese scholars.

In 1958, a "Chinese Local Chronicles Leadership Group" was established in the People's Republic of China to encourage the publication of new local chronicles. The Leadership Group issued a report entitled "Style and Structure for the Compilation of New Local Chronicles," an effort applauded by Mao Zedong and Zhou Enlai. In some provinces, committees were set up to oversee the compilation of new local chronicles, and a number of volumes appeared. Many stressed source materials; others were updates of the area for the past one hundred years. One volume on Beijing appeared, but then the Cultural Revolution was under way, local historians were attacked for crimes against the country, and the writing of local history came to an abrupt end.

Since that destructive time, local history in China has resumed. There is now a Society of Chinese Local History and Chronicles to oversee the activities of local historians. Mediating a debate between those who view chronicles as history and those who do not, the society has endorsed the position that chronicles and history are closely related and that a local chronicle is an "encyclopaedia of a place." The society issues a journal, entitled *News Bulletin of Chinese Local History and Chronicles*, and it encourages the education of its members.[6]

In England, there have been a number of efforts on behalf of local history. As noted earlier, Leicester University established a Chair of English Local History in 1952. So many local studies have been written by members of the Leicester history department, or by people who have studied there, that in 1982 the university issued a bibliography listing all such works that can be associated with that school.[7]

The Leicester histories are not all the local histories that have been published in England. Beginning late in the nineteenth century, the English undertook the publication of chronicles, various articles, and documents in a series known as the "Victoria County Histories." These continue to appear. In addition, in many localities there are local history councils that frequently issue volumes of narrative history or of documents. Throughout England, local history is often a popular subject in adult education courses offered by universities, local polytechnic schools, and local councils. In any issue of *The Local Historian*, there are lists of new local histories from all over the country.

In 1982, a report appeared on "the pattern of interest, activity, and of study in local history in England and Wales." The committee that drafted the report was asked to make recommendations about the support and services needed by amateur and professional local historians. The report revealed considerable growth of interest in local history during the past thirty years and an expansion of the needs of local historians. Among the recommendations were guidance on how groups of people could work together to produce local studies; training for those who teach local history in schools, higher education, or adult classes; and support and education for those adults, either individuals or groups, who are interested in undertaking studies of their own communities. The committee recommended that a nationally approved qualification in local history would be advisable because it would help individuals and would enhance the reputation of local history among academics.[8]

The committee also stated that a "strong, independent, national organization was needed" to champion the cause of local history in England. Its membership should include individuals, local societies, area organizations, and educational institutions. The Standing Conference for Local History therefore ceased to function in 1982 and was replaced by the British Association for Local History, which hopes to be a more activist organization on behalf of local history and local historians. Its main concern will be education, and BALH, as it is known, has taken over the publication *The Local Historian* from the Standing Conference. It is probably too soon to tell whether the new association will accomplish its goals, but it was launched with vigor and good intentions.

Bettie Miller, general secretary of the new association, has noted:

The vitality of local history in Britain during the past thirty years has come from a partnership which has existed between innumerable ordinary people seeking to understand the past history of the place in which they live and full-time historians who have not been too proud nor too aloof to help, and to seek help from the "amateurs." *The Local Historian* has played an important part in fostering this partnership in many ways, not least by its encouragement of so many new approaches to history. There will be a greater need than ever in the next thirty years for a voice which will moderate academic arrogance while improving the quality of the ordinary local historian's work.[9]

Miller believes that the cooperation between *The Local Historian* and the British Association for Local History will provide that voice.

Canada supplies another example of how local history and local historians function. There are a great many local histories of communities in Ontario, so many that they have been called as numerous as "the sand on the seashore." Many are published by local historical societies; others by individuals; some with the assistance of the provincial government. In addition, the Women's Institute in Ontario sponsors the production of local histories, called "Tweedsmuir Histories," which are partially written accounts and partially scrapbooks of information about everyday aspects of life. These are published locally, and they circulate to a wider audience on microfilm.[10] Canadian local history seems nearest to the situation that we find in the United States today.

Just what is the current condition of local history in the United States? From all indications, local history in this country is alive and well. It has been nourished, over the past twenty years, and the definition of local history has expanded to include more practitioners than simply "little old ladies in tennis shoes." This nourishment has come from a variety of sources.

Academic historians in large numbers discovered local history sometime in the 1960s, and ever since then graduate students and some university professors have issued rich volumes chronicling the past of American communities.[11] They devised new methodologies that enabled researchers to investigate community life, and they issued any number of community studies. The work generated in academe, however, has not been translated to the local scene. One professor of history complained to me that his important study of a small American city, which is cited frequently in other academic works, has sold barely half a dozen copies to people in the city about which he wrote.

Academic interest in local history is important, and academic work will eventually help to improve the writing and the perception of local history in this country. But the academics' "discovery" of local history is not the major reason for its present popularity. Rather, that popularity is derived from a number of forces that have come together to focus on America's hometowns. Eliot Wigginton and his *Foxfire* books were one cause, the historic preservation movement another. *Foxfire* took a look at the folkways of everyday people, and students in grade schools recorded how people worked and what they said. The material collected was about folk and common traditions, gathered by ordinary kids.[12]

The preservation movement looks at our domestic architecture and has jogged individuals and communities to observe our built environment closely. Houses that typify a particular style, barns, factory buildings, and even street facades have gained new importance. Prior to this, noteworthy edifices had been, in the public mind, homes of the famous and obviously outstanding architectural examples. Most people did not look at home for buildings of merit. The preservationists pointed to houses next door, and to street scenes we had long taken for granted, and our hometowns became the focus of much of their activity—and this activity, from saving local buildings to documenting a local style, generated a good deal of volunteer enthusiasm.

*Roots* has been another potent factor in the revival of interest in local history.[13] Alex Haley's family story pointed the way for genealogical pursuits among a wide range of individuals. Books appeared offering to guide people through the process of tracing their family history or their genealogical past, be they Jewish or Swedish or Dutch. The importance of *Roots* is that it democratized genealogy in areas where such study had been perceived as elitist and reinforced the trend established by *Foxfire* and the preservation movement.

Major credit for a renewal of interest in local history must also go to the Bicentennial celebration of the mid-1970s, for it continued this decentralizing trend by dividing the American experience into its varied parts. The most meaningful celebrations of the Bicentennial—aside, perhaps, from the dramatic arrival of the "tall ships" in New York Harbor—were the pageants, displays, lectures, books, exhibits, and ceremonies put on in America's communities. During the Centennial celebration in 1876, the nation had focused on the exhibits at Philadelphia. Nonetheless, Americans were urged to go forth from that gala display and write the history of America's hometowns. This they did in great number. The Bicentennial spawned this same interest once again in the history of our localities, and Bicentennial histories, or histories begun during the era of the Bicentennial, are still pouring forth from presses all over the country.

There are a number of other factors that should be taken into account when toting up the causes for the current popularity of local history. There has been a growing concern about the environment, and Americans have attempted to protect it and preserve it. The environment in question was not only located in special parcels designated as national parks, but it was everywhere, from the East Coast to the West. Federal money, too, played a part, as funds from the National Endowment for the Humanities supported projects all over the country and preservation dollars went to projects in places great and small. State humanities councils have distributed federal monies to localities.

As each of these factors came into play, it brought along its own adherents, and so local history began to be spelled out or acted out in a multitude of ways. The definition of local history now includes historical studies, preservation, urban renewal, collection of documents, architectural history, folklore studies, genealogy and family history, community development, and local boosterism.

The attraction of local history, it has been suggested, is its social and recreational role, or its capacity to generate pride of place. For some individuals it has provided a sense of tradition in a mobile society where geographic dislocations are common. In 1979, an English Committee to Review Local History suggested that the growth and popularity of local history is "rooted in social and psychological needs brought on by rapid change in environment and life style," which has brought about disruptions of older, comfortable patterns.[14]

Others have noted more mundane reasons for local history's new status, reasons that are nonetheless compelling. Its popularity, according to one writer, is the result of more people attending adult edu-

cation classes, of greater education among the population, of leisure time, of increased availability of records, and of newly discovered— and therefore potentially exciting—materials. All these factors, suggests Clive Holmes, an English historian, have caused a redefinition of the purpose and scope of local history.[15] This revival of local history that we are enjoying at present is the result of a number of complex factors that, strung together, have caused the democratization of the subject and a diversification of routes of approach.

How would one characterize the practice of local history in the United States? Statements such as those about Norway, Japan, and England cannot be made about local historians in this country. To generalize about so large a nation, with so many diverse ways of approaching the history of a community, would be to offer partial explanations. Yet there are no surveys of local historians that I know of, and so generalizations are all it is possible to offer. Local history is practiced by a great number of people in this country, and by growing numbers of academic historians. There are more and more people involved with the administration and the exhibition of local history in our communities, in addition to local historians who generally collect and preserve it and inform their fellow townspeople. Many of the local historians I meet are young, well educated, and willing to work hard. They care about doing a good job. Granted, there are still local historians who read little, research inadequately, and write badly, and there will probably always be such people. But the "little old lady in tennis shoes" is probably wearing athletic footware to help her get about all the faster. The local historians I meet have great desire to do a "good job." I sense a hustle and a purposefulness in the field.

❧

There are striking differences between the situation of local history in the United States and what we find elsewhere. In many other countries, there is a sense of common direction that is missing here. In other countries, I am pleasantly surprised by the sense that efforts by local historians are clearly seen as contributing to general, national

knowledge. This might be because other places are smaller or more homogeneous, but that is not true of China, with its vast area and diverse peoples. This sense of common purpose, then, is not a function of size. It may, however, be due to a greater respect on the part of some nations for what local history can and should be. Thus Norway and China and England have journals aimed at educating and informing their amateur historians, and in England there has been talk of instituting a national training program for local historians.

Whatever the reason, local historians in many other settings appear to have more official services aimed at them, more education directed at their needs, more conferences that include them and arrange for discussions of their problems. While the situation in the United States is different in each and every state, and indeed in every community, there does not seem to be the "care and feeding" of amateur local historians here that can be found elsewhere.

This situation need not continue, however, and it is the local historian him- or herself who can best alter it. Rather than wait for a national organization to shepherd our cause, or for state departments of education to come to our aid, it might be best if local historians became activists for the things that would serve them best. If regional meetings of local historians are not presently held, they can easily be established under the aegis of a historical society or community college. If avenues of publication are hard to find, then discussions with editors of historical journals might clarify what types of articles they seek and publish. If meetings of whatever associations we look to for guidance do not include sessions that interest local historians, then the committees who set up annual meetings should be contacted and informed of that fact and suggestions offered. Every request we make for aid will not be answered, but gradually the voices of America's local historians will begin to be heard; and gradually, yes, but surely, those needs will begin to be met.

There are any number of writers who are happy to list the sins of local historians, and there are others who have established guide-

lines for us to follow. Some of their suggestions are valuable; others miss the mark or are couched in such a way that they are relatively useless to the amateur delving into a community's past. Rather than rehash old lists, I propose one of my own. Its contents have been stated in one way or another in other parts of the book; as a finale, they are here gathered together and rephrased as my suggestions to local historians who want to do the very best they can in telling, or retelling, the history of their hometowns.

*1. Read.* Read for knowledge of the particular, read for an introduction to new ways of looking at the past and for new questions to ask of it. Read widely for breadth. Read to understand the context of your story so that a local history or local history project can be placed in its historical setting. Read to know what is unique and what is not. Read to learn of comparable situations and of neighboring events. Put your own historical work in context.

*2. Recognize the plurality of the past.* Look for the many histories that make up the past of your particular place. Be alert to all the voices and experiences that make up the fabric of a single community. Consider historical investigation the process of adding to what is known, not limiting the past to what has already been said. Question the standard story—not to prove it false, but to amplify it. Begin any investigation by asking as many questions about the topic as you can think of and then pursue answers in as many ways, and in as many places, as possible. Do not forget that local materials can often be found outside of a locality.

*3. Be responsible.* Our responsibility is twofold: to the past and to the future. We must thoroughly investigate our subjects; we must read what the sources tell us with an open mind; we must not let individual facts stand without explaining their place in our story. We are responsible to the future, so our pathway through the sources must be made clear by full, accurate, and helpful footnotes. Remember the historian's golden rule: "leave footnotes unto others as you would have footnotes left unto you."

*4. Write to be read.* So much local history is collected and published but not read, partly because so much local history is dreadfully written. Write your local history with the expectation that people in the community will read it. If they do not, it is because you have failed to be lively, clear, interesting, and informative. When writing a local history, it is often helpful to write for a particular reader. Then read your history with an eye and ear to what that reader will want to know, what that reader will need to have explained. Do not overload a reader with information that you feel is particularly important without telling the reader why you have provided such detail. Do not get so bogged down with facts that they are presented without being explained. Think of the reasons why historical fiction is successful. Novels are usually well plotted and clearly written. There is a lesson here for local historians.

5. *Consider diversity.* There are many ways of presenting the material of local history. Do not be so intent upon one form — a complete written history, for example — that you neglect other forms more suitable to your material. Short newspaper pieces are sometimes the best way of presenting episodes that would clutter a larger historical work. Exhibits and exhibit brochures are sometimes better formats for specific information than are books. Displays in city halls or chambers of commerce or local churches are sometimes a good way of expanding the audience for local history. A historical talk at a community center might attract people who do not visit the historical society. Think about the diverse forms that local history can take, and of the many audiences there are for it. Consider the electronic media as an outlet for local history. Think about using teamwork to accomplish what would take one individual a lifetime.

6. *Provide for the reader or viewer.* Anticipate the questions that a reader might have. Provide a map, explain a chart, explain where a particular piece of history is heading so the reader knows what to expect. When mounting exhibits, make sure that there is adequate information to explain the objects and pictures displayed. Look at your material from the viewpoint of someone who is curious but who does not have your background. Think about ways of making your presentation as clear as possible.

7. *Think about today.* All local history is not origins, as interesting as local historians have always found origins to be. Today will soon be the past, too. Therefore, collect materials from the present. Salt the archives with contemporary data. Encourage people to write memoirs, keep diaries, write and save letters; and make sure that historical materials are clearly marked so they they end up in area archives. Consider yourself a source of contemporary history, and write your recollections of living in your community, of town trials, of special events, of everyday life. Think about the things that you would like to discover if you were a future historian of our own time, and attempt to provide information that would be helpful. Can you document a local election? Do you photograph flood damage or building renovation or removal? Do you encourage others to do so?

8. *Seek advice.* There are many people "out there" who have information that will help you be a better informed or more talented local historian. Ask editors what constitutes an acceptable article; take classes in history and anthropology and sociology at a community college; request that the local historical society set up meetings of local historians or provide seminars for them; question why articles on local history do not appear regularly in the journals you read; let the historical organizations to which you belong know that you need assistance on certain topics; look up local experts, and regional ones too, to help clarify the material on which you are working; take part in the organization of the associations you need to help you do a better job. Represent the interests of local historians everywhere; our material is different, but our concerns and our working conditions are very much the same.

Finally, enjoy. There is no need to mandate this. Enjoy what you do, for local history is fun. And local history is also lasting—it is one of the few forms of knowledge that is sure to have a local impact, that will be kept and referred to in the future and will be around long after any of us. Look at the local history materials you use today: some are good sources, others weak; some well prepared, others poorly presented. But they have been preserved, and they represent a real contribution to what a community thinks about itself. To be a local historian is to make a contribution that endures. What more can any of us ask?

## NOTES

1. Johan Huizinga, "The Task of Cultural History," in Huizinga, *Men and Ideas: History, the Middle Ages, the Renaissance*, translated by James S. Holmes and Hans van Marle (1929; New York: Meridian Books, 1959), 21.

2. Rolf Fladby, "The Norwegian Institute for Local History and Local History Research," *The Local Historian* 11 (November 1974): 217-224.

3. Eija Kennerley, "Local History in Finland," *The Local Historian* 12 (November 1976): 149-151.

4. Keith Brown, *Shinjo: The Chronicle of a Japanese Village*, Ethnology Monograph No. 2 (Pittsburgh: University Center for International Studies, University of Pittsburgh, 1979), 32.

5. *Ibid.*, 31

6. Meng-bie Zhang, "Current Trends in the Study and Publication of Local Chronicles in China" (unpublished paper, 1985); and Albert Feuerwerker, ed., *Chinese Social and Economic History from the Song to 1900: A Report of the American Delegation to a Sino-American Symposium, Beijing, 26 October-1 November 1980*, Michigan Monographs in Chinese Studies 45 (Ann Arbor: Center for Chinese Studies, University of Michigan, 1982).

7. *The Local Historian* 15 (February 1982): 62-63.

8. *The Local Historian* 14 (August 1981): 446-448.

9. *The Local Historian* 15 (May 1982): 123-124, and 15 (August 1982): 191.

10. Royce MacGillivray, "Local History as a Form of Popular Culture in Ontario," *New York History* 65 (October 1984): 367-377.

11. Kathleen Neils Conzen, "Community Studies, Urban History, and American Local History," in Michael Kammen, ed., *The Past Before Us* (Ithaca, New York: Cornell University Press, 1980), 270-292.

12. Eliot Wigginton, editor, *The Foxfire Book* (Garden City, New York: Anchor Books, Doubleday & Co., 1972).

13. Alex Haley, *Roots* (New York: Alfred A. Knopf, 1976).

14. "Summary of Report: Committee to Review Local History," *The Local Historian* 13 (November 1979): 451-456.

15. Clive Holmes, *Seventeenth-Century Lincolnshire* (Lincoln: History of Lincolnshire Committee for the Society for Lincolnshire History and Archaeology, 1980), 1-5.

# INDEX